THE SANTA FE TRAIL
YESTERDAY AND TODAY

THE SANTA FE TRAIL
YESTERDAY AND TODAY

by

William E. Hill

Cover Design by Teresa Sales

The CAXTON PRINTERS, Ltd.
Caldwell, Idaho
1992

Library of Congress Cataloging-in-Publication Data

Hill, William E.
    The Santa Fe Trail, yesterday and today / William E. Hill.
        p.   cm.
    Includes bibliographical references (p.   ) and index.
    ISBN 0-87004-354-4   : $12.95
    1. Santa Fe Trail--History.   2. Santa Fe Trail--Guidebooks.
    I. Title.
    F787.H52   1992
    978--dc20   92-13064
                                                        CIP

Lithographed and bound in the United States of America by
The CAXTON PRINTERS, Ltd.
Caldwell, ID 83605
155383

Dedication

To my wife, Jan, for her understanding, willingness, bravery, and genuine enthusiasm during our honeymoon trip exploring the Santa Fe Trail and during subsequent summer trips on the trails west. To my son, Will, who has grown up spending his summers bouncing over trail ruts, climbing up and down hills, and who was there whenever help was needed.

Contents

Illustrations ix

Preface xiii

Acknowledgements xv

Introduction xvii

Part I: Early History of the Santa Fe Trail 1

Part II: Maps—Guides—Diaries 31

Part III: Pictorial Journey—Yesterday and Today 101

Part IV: Museums and Displays 201

Part V: Background 213

            Recommended Reading 214

            Bibliography 219

Index 225

Illustrations

Brown's Notebook Pages 34-47
Brown's Map 48-49
Map of the Western Territory 50
Gregg's Map 51
Map: New Mexico and the Southern Rocky Mountains 52-53
Lieutenant Emory's Map 54
Official Kansas Highway Map 55
Santa Fe Spring 104
Arrow Rock Tavery 104
Fort Osage 105
Fort Osage Today 105
Fort Leavenworth Drawing 106
Fort Leavenworth Today 106
Fort Leavenworth - The Rookery 107
Fort Leavenworth - Santa Fe Trail Ruts 107
Westport Landing 108
Westport Landing Today 108
Independence Square 109
Independence Square Today 109
Independence Spring and Cabin 110
Brady Cabin Today 110
Independence Log Courthouse 111
Alexander Majors' Home 111
National Frontier Trails Center 112
Shawnee Mission Today 113
Minor Park Swale 114
Rolling Prairie 115
Council Oak Today — Council Grove 116
Conn Store — Council Grove 117
Conn Store Today 117
Kaw Mission Today 118
Last Chance Store Today 118
Cow Creek 119
Cow Creek Today 119
Pawnee Rock 120
Early Photo of Pawnee Rock 121
Pawnee Rock Today 121
Indian Lookout 122
Pawnee Rock View Today 122

Pawnee Fork 123
Pawnee Fork Today 123
Fort Larned — Oldest Photo 124
Fort Larned Today 124
Fort Larned — Junior Officers' Quarters 125
Fort Larned — Junior Officers' Quarters Today 125
Fort Larned — Commanding Officer's Quarters 126
Fort Larned — Commanding Officer's Quarters Today 126
Prairie Dog Town 127
Prairie Dog Town 128
Prairie Dog Town Today 128
Fort Dodge 129
Fort Dodge Today 129
Buffalo 130
Buffalo Today 130
Big Timber 131
Big Timber Today 132
Bent's Fort — Exterior 133
Bent's Fort — Exterior Today 133
Bent's Fort — Exterior (Abert) 134
Bent's Fort — Exterior (Doniphan) 134
Bent's Fort Today (two photos) 135
Bent's Fort — Interior 136
Bent's Fort — Interior Today 136
Spanish Peaks 137
Spanish Peaks Today 137
Spanish Peaks 138
Spanish Peaks Today 138
Raton Mountains 139
Raton Today 140
Raton Zigzag 141
Raton Today 141
Crossing the Arkansas 142
Arkansas River Today 142
Fording the Arkansas 143
The Arkansas Today 143
Indians on the Arkansas 144
Arkansas Today 144
Indian Alarm on the Cimarron River 145
Cimarron Valley Today 145
Wagon Bed Springs Today 146
Autograph Rock 146

McNees Crossing Today 147
Rabbit Ears Today 147
Approaching Round Mound 148
Round Mound View 148
Round Mound View 149
Rock Crossing Canadian Today 149
Livery Stable 150
Livery Stable Today 150
Wagon Mound Today 151
Trail Ruts Today 151
Old Fort Union 152
Old Fort Union — View Today 152–153
Mechanics' Corral (two photos) 154
Mechanics' Coral Today (two photos) 155
Fort Union Officers' Row Photo 156
Fort Union Officers' Row Today 156
Prairie (two drawings) 157
Prairie Today (two photos) 158
San Miguel Del Vado 159
San Miguel Today 159
San Miguel Church 160
San Miguel Church Today 160
Pecos Ruins 161
Pecos Ruins Today 161
Pecos Cathedral 162
Pecos Cathedral Ruins Today 162
Pecos Cathedral Ruins 163
Pecos Cathedral Today 163
Pecos Ruins — Old Photo 164
Pecos Ruins Today 164
Pigeon's Ranch Overview — Old Photo 166
Pigeon's Ranch Today 167
Pigeon's Ranch House 168
Pigeon's Ranch Building Today 169
Arrival at Santa Fe 170
Santa Fe in 1846 171
Santa Fe — Old Photo 171
Santa Fe Today 172
Santa Fe Square — Old Photo 173
Santa Fe Square Today 173
Old Map of Santa Fe 174–175
Governor's Palace — Old Photo 176

Governor's Palace Today 176
San Miguel Chapel — Old Photo 177
San Miguel Chapel Today 177
San Miguel Chapel — Old Photo 178
San Miguel Chapel Today 179
San Francisco Street — Old Photo 180
San Francisco Street — Old Drawing 180
San Francisco Street Today (two photos) 181
Old Parish Church 182
St. Francis Cathedral Today 182
Road to Taos 183
Taos Pueblo 183
Highway to Taos 184
Taos Pueblo Today 184
Jedediah Smith 185
Kit Carson 186
Charles Bent 187
William Bent 188
Josiah Gregg 189
Susan Magoffin 190
Samuel Magoffin 191
Uncle Dick Wootton 192
General Stephen Watts Kearny 193
Alexander Majors 194
Caught in the Snow 195
Snowbound Camp Today 195
Advertisement — Wagon 196
Advertisement — Store 196
Santa Fe Freight Wagon 197
Emigrant Wagon 197
Conestoga Wagon 198
Santa Fe Wagon Camp 198
Grave Today 199
Bent's Fort — Abert's Floor Plan 199

Preface

Scarcely a day passes without my experiencing a pang of regret that I am not now roving at large upon the western plains.

Josiah Gregg

There have been many things in my life that I have striven to forget, but not those journeys over the Santa Fe Trail.
My life as I look back seems to have been lived best in those days on the trail.

Marian Russell

WHAT WAS IT THAT SO MOVED THESE PEOPLE TO WRITE?

OF THE THREE great trails that headed west from the Missouri area, the Santa Fe Trail seems to have had the strongest influence on the many people who have traveled it, both yesterday and today. This book is the third in a series of books about the trails west. My first was about the Oregon Trail; the second, the California Trail; and now, the third, the Santa Fe Trail. As with Josiah Gregg, Marion Russell and Susan Magoffin who, a century and a half ago, traveled and wrote of their Santa Fe Trail experiences, the Santa Fe Trail also has had a strong beckoning call and a romantic association for me. For almost twenty years the western trails have summoned me back to them nearly every summer. Like Susan Magoffin, my wife Jan and I spent part of our honeymoon traveling down the Santa Fe Trail. Whereas Susan continued on to Chihuahua after a short stay in Santa Fe, Jan and I continued on to California after a short stay in Santa Fe. For Josiah Gregg, his first trip down the Santa Fe Trail was recommended for medical reasons. For me, my trips west provide a healthful break from the hectic schedule and pressures of teaching in the crowded, fast-paced east. All of us have memories of experiences which could never be forgotten.

My head is filled with stories about the Santa Fe Trail. Events from the past often would come alive as my family and I drove along the trail with a diary in hand. In her diary Susan Magoffin was describing the beautiful Kansas prairie with all its pretty flowers. Within minutes of reading that passage, the prairie along the side of the road was full of yellow flowers. We stopped to take a picture and then re-read the diary. Later, while crossing the Raton Mountains we saw a large brown bear rambling down the mountain crossing the trail. It reminded me of the story of Wild Bill Hickok's encounter and fight with a grizzly bear while he was crossing the Raton.

As with my two other books, this is written as an introduction to the Santa Fe Trail experience. It is for the tourist, the armchair traveler, and the history buff. It provides the reader with basic information and an overview of the whole period of the trail, from its birth with William Becknell to its final days with the completion of the railroad. Various topics are discussed and examined and a unique pictorial section is included. Read about what the traders and emigrants experienced as expressed in their own words. See the sites as they were recorded and as they appear today.

Come along now and relive the Santa Fe Trail experience.

Acknowledgements

Two simple words that say so much: "Thank You!"

There have been many people who have helped to make this project possible. Special appreciation is expressed to all the farmers, foremen, and ranchers who let us walk and drive along the trail as it crossed their properties. Many gave us permission and most gave us time from their busy workday to point out trail sites, to tell us stories about the trail, or to provide us with some cool water and shade during the hot day. In particular, Ed and Jan Boyd, Dan and Carol Sharp, Jim and Johnny Sue MacDonald, Joel and Carol McDaniels, and Dan Kipp were all very helpful.

All of us are indebted to organizations such as the national and state park systems, various local historical groups and especially to the Santa Fe Trail Association and the Oregon-California Trails Association that have been developed to safeguard the remnants and to keep the history of the trails alive.

To all the librarians at libraries big and small. Their interest was genuine, their assistance was, at times, neverending. To those librarians at the Middle Country Library who have helped over the years without always knowing the results of their assistance, a gracious, "Thank You."

Introduction

WHEN ONE THINKS of the way west, the Oregon, California and Santa Fe Trails come to mind. But when one thinks of the Santa Fe Trail itself, high adventure, fortunes and romance come to mind. While there are a great many similarities among the trails, there are many characteristics that distinguish the Santa Fe Trail from the other two great trails.

The Santa Fe is the oldest of the three. It was in constant use from 1821 until 1880 when the railroad replaced it. During the 1840s and 1850s when the Oregon and the California Trails were opened, Independence, Westport, and Fort Leavenworth were used as some of their jumping-off places. By then, the Santa Fe Trail, which had been using these same areas for many years, was already in its prime. The route to Santa Fe was well established and the trail was a fine beaten path. When the wagon routes to Oregon and California were being blazed from Independence, they started down the well-defined Santa Fe Trail before branching off to the northwest, near present day Gardner, Kansas, to cut their new route west. Thus, for the first forty miles west of Independence, all three trail systems coincided.

While the Oregon and California Trails were used at first by emigrants seeking new lands for their homes and families, and then briefly by the gold-seeking argonauts of 1849, the Santa Fe Trail was originally developed as a route for commerce between Mexico and the United States. Most of the major developments of the trail concerning its rise and fall were associated with trade and commerce. However, during the California Gold Rush of 1849 and the Colorado Gold Rush of 1859, parts of the Santa Fe Trail were also used by gold seekers. Some California bound gold seekers who feared that the Platte

River trails would be too crowded and the grass would be too scarce for their stock took the trail to Santa Fe. Then they continued to California via either the Old Spanish Trail or the Gila route. In 1859, "Pike's Peak or Bust" became a familiar sign seen along the Santa Fe Trail.

For the first twenty-five years of the trail's history Santa Fe lay in a foreign country, situated on the other side of dangerous Indian territory. There was little first hand contact between Americans and Mexicans. The stories that did reach the United States told of an exotic land, with men and women with a different culture and customs, and of huge profits that could be made. Oregon and California were also situated far across Indian territory, but only during the first years when a few emigrant parties migrated to California was it part of a foreign land. Oregon, with its stories of furs and the rich Willamette Valley, lay in lands claimed by both the United States and Britain. Events that began in 1846 soon brought all three areas, New Mexico, California, and Oregon under the flag of the United States.

The nature of the commerce carried on the Santa Fe Trail varied over its history. Santa Fe was originally an outpost on the Mexican frontier far from the government in Mexico City. Goods that were sent to Santa Fe were generally of poorer quality and very costly. Santa Fe was yearning for new and better goods. Much of the commerce during the early years was directly related to the Indian and fur trade that operated out of Taos and Santa Fe. Many of the earliest individuals involved in the trade considered themselves to be trappers and traders. William Becknell's trip to Santa Fe in 1821 had originally been organized to trade with the Indians in Colorado. Upon hearing of Mexican independence, Becknell headed for Santa Fe and the Santa Fe trade began! Some recent historians feel he was actually headed for Santa Fe all the time. Little is known of the actual goods Becknell carried, but his advice to other later traders was to bring calicos and ". . . goods of excellent quality and unfaded colors." Meredith M. Marmaduke's caravan of 1824 carried cotton goods, woolen goods, cutlery, silk shawls and looking glasses. He returned with some Spanish dollars, gold and silver bullion, beaver furs and a few mules. As fur trapping declined and the Mexicans allowed the Missouri traders to travel to Mexican territory, the type of goods traded changed. By the 1840s, James J. Webb described the typical goods traded in Santa Fe as a wide variety of dry goods, including cottons, woolens and silks of solid, striped, or plaid patterns and various colors; notions such as, buttons, threads, hooks and eyes, combs, needles and pins; and hardware including nails, spoons, scissors, knives, saws, hoes, and spades. Under Spanish and Mexican rule goods such as gun powder, shoes and boots, clothing and tobacco were considered contraband and were not allowed into Mexican territory.

The vast extent of commerce during the trail's first twenty-two years was recorded by Josiah Gregg, a well-known trader on the Santa Fe Trail. The following table is from his *Commerce Of The Prairies*.

Some general statistics of the Santa Fe Trade may prove not wholly without interest to the merchantile reader. With this view, I have prepared the following table of the probable amounts of merchandise invested in the Santa Fe Trade, from 1822 to 1843 inclusive, and about the portion of the same transferred to the Southern markets (chiefly Chihuahua) during the same period; together with the approximate number of wagons, men and proprietors engaged each year:

Years	Amt. Mdse.	W'gs.	Men.	Pro's.	T'n to Ch'a.	Remarks
1822	15,000		70	60		Pack-animals only used.
1823	12,000		50	30		do. do.
1824	35,000	26	100	80	3,000	do. and wagons.
1825	65,000	37	130	90	5,000	do. do.
1826	90,000	60	100	70	7,000	Wagons only henceforth.
1827	85,000	55	90	50	8,000	
1828	150,000	100	200	80	20,000	3 men killed, being the first.
1829	60,000	30	50	20	5,000	1st E.S. Es.—1 trader killed.
1830	120,000	70	140	60	20,000	First oxen used by traders.
1831	250,000	130	320	80	80,000	Two men killed.
1832	140,000	70	150	40	50,000	⎰ Party defeated on Canadian
1833	180,000	105	185	60	80,000	⎱ 2 men killed, 3 perished.
1834	150,000	80	160	50	70,000	2d U.S. Escort.
1835	140,000	75	140	40	70,000	
1836	130,000	70	135	35	60,000	
1837	150,000	80	160	35	80,000	
1838	90,000	50	100	20	40,000	
1839	250,000	130	250	40	100,000	Arkansas Expedition.
1840	50,000	30	60	5	10,000	Chihuahua Expedition.
1841	150,000	60	100	12	80,000	Texan Santa Fe Expedition.
1842	160,000	70	120	15	90,000	
1843	450,000	230	350	30	300,000	3d U.S. Es.—Ports closed.

As the years progressed and the nature of the commerce changed, the value of the commerce taken to Santa Fe and beyond increased even more. What had started out involving only a few thousand dollars became worth hundreds of thousands of dollars. The value of commerce was rapidly growing when Gregg's records stopped. The value of goods and money brought back east was even greater. In 1824, Meredith Marmaduke and others were reported to have returned from their venture to Santa Fe with furs valued at $180,000. Thirty-five years later in 1859 the value of commerce was placed at over $10,000,000 and by 1862 one estimate put the value of commerce at $40,000,000. Firms as far east as Pittsburgh and New York were involved both indirectly or directly with the Santa Fe trade. Some traders used wagons produced in Pittsburgh and obtained goods from New York.

In the earliest years, most of those engaged in the trade along the trail were individual properietors. After 1828 that was no longer true, and by 1843 only one in ten were. And after the Mexican War that figure was reduced even more as professional freighters began contracting to haul the goods. The most famous freighting firms were: Ben Holladay; Russell, Majors, and Waddell; Jones and Cartwright; and Byram Brothers.

As more and more traders became lured to the riches identified with the Santa Fe trade, wider markets were required in order to sell all the goods being transported. By 1824, some of the traders continued south to Chihauhau. As shown in Gregg's table [preceding], by 1835 half of all the merchandise went there. Thus, the end of the trail was extended deeper into Mexican territory, and the trail to Santa Fe represented only half of the trip. Susan Magoffin's 1846 journey with her husband, Santa Fe trader Samuel Magoffin, to Santa Fe and Chihauhau is recorded in her diary.

After the United States defeated Mexico in 1846, Santa Fe became part of the United States. Much of the traffic along the trail was associated with the military occupation and expansion of its influence in the southwest. Professional freighters became more and more active. Alexander Majors switched from hauling predominantly commercial goods for civilians to hauling freight for the military. As more settlers moved to the southwest, more consumer goods from the east were transported over the Santa Fe Trail. The range of consumer goods widened to include major furniture and household items.

Although traffic did move both east and west over the Oregon and California Trails, those trails were developed primarily as westward routes for emigrants. Traffic on the Santa Fe Trail from its inception was two way. While the heaviest traffic moved westward, merchants and traders sent goods in both directions from each end of the trail. In addition to gold and silver, furs, mules and wool were some of the major items brought back east. Traders frequently sold most of their wagons and stock in Santa Fe and then returned east with only those wagons needed to carry the goods being transported. Once back, they purchased new wagons, stock, and trade goods and started the whole process all over again. Thus, outfitting became a constant and major business for the jumping-off towns. As professional freighters became the dominant users of the Santa Fe Trail, it was economically necessary for them to haul goods both east and west.

The length of the Santa Fe Trail was much shorter than that of either the Oregon or California Trail systems. The Oregon and California Trails were both about 2,000 miles but varied based on the specific starting point and final destinations. Depending on the specific jumping-off site and the specific route taken to Santa Fe, the distance over it also varied. The distance from Independence to Santa Fe using the Mountain Branch was about 835 miles, while the distance using the Cimarron Cutoff was about 780 miles. However, because of the greater problems associated with the Cimarron Cutoff and the growing settlements along the Mountain Branch, the longer route came to be used more. After the Civil War, when construction moved the railroad constantly westward, the eastern terminus of the Santa Fe Trail moved west with it. The railroad, also, more closely followed the Mountain Branch. The length of the

Santa Fe Trail was constantly being shortened until 1880, when the last thirty miles of track were finished. Then people and goods could move more quickly and safely all the way from Missouri to Santa Fe by train. Then the trail was no more.

Because the length of the trail systems differed greatly, the usage and time required for travel over the trail systems also differed. All those heading west on any of the trail systems had to wait for the spring grasses to appear. However, those going to Oregon or California had to leave no later than June, while those journeying to Santa Fe could leave at almost any time from April to August or September and still make it safely to Santa Fe and back before being caught by some of the terrible snow storms. Some Santa Fe traders tried to extend the trading season too much and were not always so lucky. In 1841, two caravans led by Antonio Robidoux and Manuel Alvarez lost both men and mules in a November blizzard near Cottonwood Crossing. In 1844, Albert Speyer's caravan was caught in a blizzard near Willow Bar on the Cimarron and lost most of its mules. For years following that, travelers and traders stopping in the area entertained themselves by arranging and rearranging the bones into strange and fantastic shapes. In 1848, George Brewerton reported seeing a large circle formed by mule skulls there. (The area soon became known as "Mule Head" due to all the skeleton remains of the mules.) Over the years other traders were also caught at various other locations along the trail by the terrible blizzards that descended on the plains.

Normally, most traders could easily make it to Santa Fe and back all within the year. In 1831, the caravan Josiah Gregg traveled with left Missouri in mid-May, made it to Santa Fe in just over two months, and returned to Independence in early October. By the late 1840s, many caravans were making the westward trip in less than two months. By the 1850s, some freighters were even making two successful trips in a year. Probably the fastest trader on the Santa Fe Trail was Francis X. Aubry. In both 1848 and 1851 Aubry was able to take three caravans to Santa Fe. In 1848, his caravans to Santa Fe left in March, June, and September. That same year, riding alone, Aubry set the record for traveling from Santa Fe to Independence in a few hours less than six days. He was known along the Trail for his record-breaking trips. Not until the advent of the Pony Express were similar feats of speed and endurance accomplished by a single rider. The usual rate of speed for the large caravans, however, was about fifteen to twenty miles a day for a trip lasting over two months. In 1856, Uncle Dick Wootton described a typical caravan as having thirty-six wagons, with five yoke of oxen each. It required about forty men and when it was all lined up, it stretched out for about a mile. Some freighters seemed to have a flair for the artistic. In 1866, Colonel J. F. Meline reported passing wagons pulled by ten yoke of oxen with the oxen pulling each wagon, ". . . either all black, all white, all spotted or otherwise marked uniformily."

While the speed at which wagon trains traveled on the Oregon and California Trails was similar to those traveling on the Santa Fe Trail, the same length of time for travel was an impossibility for those bound for, or those returning from Oregon or California. The distance was just too great. During the 1840s, the average length of time to travel was 158 days to California and 169 to Oregon. However, some companies in the 1840s took over 200 days to complete the trip to California and/or Oregon. Because of all the improvements along the trails, a trip made in the 1850s averaged about 113 days to California and 129 days to Oregon. One of the fastest times recorded was by Lorenzo Sawyer who, in 1850, took only seventy-six days to get to California.

While the Santa Fe Trail was much shorter, that did not

make conditions necessarily easier or safer for those traveling on it. Water or the lack of it was one major problem. The crossing of the mountains also had to be contended with.

No matter which trail was used, water and grass were the crucial elements for a successful venture. These were the fuels on which the caravans depended. Without them man and beast would surely die. Therefore, all the trails followed river systems whenever possible. Some followed them for a few miles while others followed major rivers for many miles. The Oregon and California Trails joined to follow the great Platte River system and its tributaries half way across the continent to the South Pass. Then the trails followed the Bear, the Snake, and finally the Columbia rivers. The California Trail followed the Oregon Trail but left the Snake to meet the Mary's or Humbolt River system. Then it followed either the Carson or Truckee Rivers into the Sierra Nevada and into California. The Santa Fe Trail joined the Arkansas River. The Mountain Branch continued to follow the Arkansas, or its tributaries, while the Cimarron Cutoff left the Arkansas to meet and follow along the Cimarron River. Both routes then left their respective major river system to cut across the land to meet again near La Junta and to head to Santa Fe.

When the traders and emigrants could not travel along river valleys, they tried to travel from spring to spring. All the trail systems had their famous springs, and some were along the main rivers and creeks. The Oregon and California Trails had Alcove Spring, Warm Springs, and the many Emigrant Springs. The Santa Fe Trail had Diamond Spring, Lost Spring, Willow Spring, and Santa Clara Spring, to mention only a few. However, the most crucial springs were located in the dry stretches. The Oregon and California Trail systems had dry stretches such as Sublettes Flat, the Great Salt Lake Desert, the Forty Mile Deserts and the Black Rock Desert. Springs such as the ones at Pilot

Peak on the Salt Lake Desert, Rabbit Hole and Double Hot Springs on the Black Rock Desert, and Double Wells and Boiling Hot Springs on the Forty Mile Deserts became the goal and sustainer of life. The Santa Fe Trail's desert was its infamous "Jornada." This was the common term for Jornada del Muerto or Journey of Death, which was a difficult waterless passage of one day or more. Many trappers, traders and teamsters almost died while crossing the Jornada, before they reached the waters of either the Lower or Wagon Bed Spring, the Middle Spring, or the Upper Spring along the dry Cimarron. This was especially true before 1834. Jedediah Smith was killed by Indians while looking for water in 1831. In 1833 the rains were so hard and the ground so soft that the later caravan wagons using the Middle Crossing cut the trail deeply into the earth all the way across the Jornada to water and safety. They simply followed the deep ruts left by the 1833 caravan.

The Oregon Trail had its Blue Mountains and Cascades for the emigrants to struggle over; the California Trail, its Sierra Nevada; and the Santa Fe's Mountain Branch had the Raton Mountains to cross. All were major obstacles to those traveling. The routes over them were hazardous with steep grades, large rocks and boulders, and difficult stream crossings. By fall sudden snow storms had to be contended with.

On the Oregon and California Trails the mountain routes were improved shortly after the wagon trains first began traveling over them. Samuel Barlow built a toll road across the Cascades in Oregon in 1846. Businessmen in the various gold towns in California became engaged in improving the route. In 1856, businessmen from Stockton spent $5,000 on the Big Trees Route. They built eight bridges, one fourteen feet wide and seventy-five feet long, and they also straightened the road crossing the Sierra Nevada. They even sent representatives out to encourage emigrant companies to use their new route to come to their city. In 1865, late in the history of the Santa Fe Trail, "Uncle Dick" Wootton built a twenty-seven mile toll road over the Raton Mountains that finally reduced most of the hazards and time required to cross the mountains. He straightened and widened the road and blasted out the "Devil's Rock," a major hazard on the trail over the Raton which forced wagons to the steep edge of the mountainside.

Terrible winter snow storms were a constant danger in the mountains. In 1860, Alexander Majors led one of four wagon caravans that were caught in the Raton Mountains. He was forced to leave his wagons and 300 tons of supplies meant for the military and civilians of New Mexico in the mountains. He returned with his oxen to Fort Wise to wait until the winter broke before trying to continue crossing the mountains. On the California Trail, in 1846, the Donner Party, which was trying to cross the Sierra Nevada, was not so lucky. They were trapped by the deep snow. Half of the party died before the survivors were rescued the following spring.

All travelers frequently faced death caused by accident, disease, or attack. Diseases, including smallpox, typhoid, dysentery, malaria, and cholera were encountered along the trails. In 1849, cholera affected the Santa Fe trail as it did the other trails west. It was prevalent at all the jumping-off sites moving down the trail past Council Grove and out onto the plains. While the cause of cholera was not discovered until 1883 after the end of the Santa Fe Trail, the treatment for malaria was discovered by Dr. John Sappington of Arrow Rock, Missouri. Manufacture of his quinine anti-fever pills became "standard equipment" for the well-seasoned travelers and malaria did not seem to take as great a toll as it did on the northern trails. Since the Santa Fe Trail also became the stage route, "Cabin Fever" (claustrophobia) and "Coach Fever" (motion sickness) also took their tolls on the stage passengers. While not life-threatening, they did make the trip west uncomfortable for many passengers.

The loss of goods was another problem that faced prospective traders. There were the usual losses to contend with in river crossings and wagon breakdowns. Goods were also frequently used as gifts to Indians in return for safe passage through their lands. However, other situations could result in serious losses and complete disaster. At first, Santa Fe traders had to be concerned about the confiscation of their goods by Spanish authorities. Later, after Mexican independence, they had to worry about the high duties placed on their goods or wagons by the Mexican officials. Traders and travelers also feared robbers and outlaws who also preyed on them. The well-known Mexican trader Don Antonio Jose Chavez was attacked and killed in 1843 by John McDaniels and other Texan sympathizers near Lyon, Kansas. The creek where he was taken and then murdered came to be incorrectly called "Jarvis Creek," a corruption of Chavez Creek. Between 1842 and 1844, a gang of outlaws operated along the trail in an area about twenty-five miles east of Council Grove. In 1844, they robbed and killed twenty-eight Mexican traders on their way east to trade. In the 1850s, a gang of thieves operated out of La Plazarota near Ft. Union. Dick Wootton lost a wagon one evening. Luckily, he was able to track down the suspected thieves and to get his wagon back. During the Civil War, traders all along the route also had to worry about attacks by Confederate armies or guerillas. The Cimarron Cutoff was practically abandoned during the Civil War and even the stage route was switched to the Mountain Route. However, those who traveled on the Oregon and California trails had, in this respect, less to worry about, and were safer from Confederate attack during the Civil War.

It was the Indian encounters, however, that posed the greatest danger. These encounters created a much greater problem along the Santa Fe Trail than they did on either the Oregon or California Trail systems. Although the Oregon and California Trails were opened in the early 1840s, Indians did not become a serious problem to the traveler until after the Civil War. During most of the early period, Indian-emigrant encounters were largely concerned with stealing or with requests for goods as payments to allow the emigrants to cross Indian lands unharmed.

In 1823, John McKnight was the first recorded trader killed by Indians along the Santa Fe Trail. Two years later two more traders were killed. From 1828, with the death of Santa Fe traders McNees and Monroe, deaths resulting from Indian attacks were common until almost the end of the trail period. Nearly every caravan had some type of encounter with Indians. U.S. Army escorts first appeared in 1829 and then again in 1833 and 1834. By the 1860s and 1870s, Indian attacks increased dramatically, the Cheyenne and Arapaho raided the trail from the northern plains; the Kiowa and Comanche raided from the southern plains; and the Navaho and Apache raided in the southwest. Not until after the end of the Santa Fe Trail were the last Indians finally subdued by the army and forced onto reservations.

Because of hostilities from various sources the military became closely associated with the Santa Fe Trail. In 1846, the trail became the invasion route for the U.S. Army under General Kearny in the war against Mexico. Once Santa Fe was taken, part of the army containing the Mormon Battalion blazed a new route to California along the Gila River. Another part of the Army headed south from Santa Fe further into Mexican territory. Although the acquisition of the whole southwest, including both California and New Mexico, were American goals during the war, the U.S. Army had used the Santa Fe Trail, not the California Trail to invade California. Once the war was over, the Santa Fe Trail was still heavily used by the U.S. Army.

The army soon began the construction of military posts along the Santa Fe Trail to help provide constant protection for the traders from the Indians. Perhaps, this was because economic interests and trade dominated politics more than concern for the average emigrants who were now moving along the Oregon and California Trails in record numbers.

Along the Oregon Trail and California Trail systems fewer forts per mile were established than along the Santa Fe Trail. Since the Oregon and California trails coincided with each other into Utah and southeastern Idaho, many of the military forts actually served both trails. Fort Leavenworth, Old Fort Kearny (Child), Fort Kearny, Fort Grattan, Fort McPherson (Cottonwood), Camp Mitchell, Fort Laramie, Fort Caspar (Platte Bridge Station), Fort Bridger, Fort Floyd (located off the main trail), and Cantonment Loring all served both. Some of these forts, Fort Grattan and Fort Mitchell functioned for only a year or two, while others, such as Fort Laramie and Fort Bridger, served for two decades or more. Past the Idaho area, on the California Trail there was Fort Churchill. On the main Oregon Trail, Fort Dalles(Drum), Fort Cascades, Fort Vancouver, and Fort Yamhill were established to provide protection for both settler and travelers. On the Southern Oregon route Fort Hoskins, Fort Umpqua, and Fort Lane provided similar protection from the Indians.

Over the years there were sixteen main fortified cantonments or military forts that were developed along the trail to deal with the dangers associated with the Santa Fe Trail and trade. In fact, one fort, Fort Leavenworth, actually served to protect travelers on the Santa Fe, Oregon and California Trails in the eastern Kansas-

Nebraska area. Fort Riley, another fort built off the trail, served both the Santa Fe and Smoky Hill trails. Fort Osage, near the beginning of the trail, was the first fort, but it actually pre-dated the development of Santa Fe Trail. Fort Marcy was built at the end of the trail on a hill overlooking Santa Fe in 1846. Some of these forts or posts, such as Fort Mann, Fort Aubry, and Camp Nichols were active for only one year. Fort Zarah lasted only six years. Only Fort Leavenworth, Fort Marcy, Fort Larned, Fort Dodge, and Fort Lyons II lasted over fifteen years. Often another fort was built elsewhere to replace the earlier one. This was the case when Fort Leavenworth replaced Fort Osage in the eastern Kansas-Missouri area. In central Kansas in the Arkansas Valley, Camp on Pawnee Fort became known as Camp Alert, was moved a few miles and became Fort Larned. Its adobe building were later rebuilt in stone. Fort Mann, then Fort Atkinson, and later, Fort Dodge were located in the same general area and successively replaced each other as the protector of trade in southwestern Kansas. Fort Wise, Fort Lyon I, and Fort Lyon II in eastern Colorado followed a similar pattern. There were even three different Fort Unions built in the same location. In addition, other forts, such as Fort Ellsworth, were constructed near the trail, and various trading posts were also established on the trail.

Another interesting difference among the trail systems was the development of different wagons which came to be associated with the different trails. Although emigrants are often depicted in the larger Conestoga wagons commonly used in the east for hauling freight, most present-day historians generally agree that the emigrants going west did not use the Conestoga wagons. The emigrants on the Oregon and California Trails tended to use smaller farm type wagons. The typical emigrant wagons usually had only five or six wagon bows, but larger ones had as many as eight. The usual distance between the bows was about two feet. The wagon bed was flat and had nearly square or perpendicular ends. The width was standardized at either thirty-eight or forty-two inches. The side boards for the box were twelve, fourteen, or sixteen inches. If a second board was added, it was usually ten or twelve inches. The typical box depth was between twelve and twenty-eight inches. The front wheels on nearly all wagons were smaller which enabled the wagons to turn a little. The wheels on the farm wagons ranged in height from thirty-eight to forty-four inches for the front ones, with the larger rear wheels ranging from forty to fifty-six inches. The front wheels had twelve spokes while the rear wheels had fourteen.

As the history of the Santa Fe Trail unfolded a variety of wagons came to be associated with it during its different periods of growth. The few emigrants who traveled over the Santa Fe Trail used the smaller farm wagons common to the Oregon and California Trails, but it was the freight wagons which came to dominate and symbolize the Santa Fe Trail. While there appears to have been no one single wagon that dominated the whole period of the Santa Fe trade, there were some that seem to have been widely used during different times.

The freight wagons most commonly used on the Santa Fe Trail were much larger and more colorful than the emigrant wagons. Many were similar in size to the Conestoga Wagons, but did not have the curved shape box and raked ends with the distinctive taller wagon bows at each end. While there is still debate among historians regarding how widespread the use of Conestoga wagons was, there is sufficient evidence to indicate that some Conestoga wagons were used to haul freight over the Santa Fe Trail in the earlier years. According to Josiah Gregg and others, some Pittsburgh or Conestoga type wagons were used on the Santa Fe Trail during the 1830s and 1840s. Also, the color combinations described on some Santa Fe wagons were typical of the eastern Conestoga wagons. When the demand for freight wagons was great, and before their were enough wagon makers in the west to meet demand, a wide variety of wagons, including the Conestoga Wagons, appears to have been used on the Santa Fe Trail.

The term "Murphy Wagon" is most frequently used to describe the Santa Fe Trail type wagons that were developed and used by the mid-1840s and later. These wagons were built in the "west" in St. Louis and in the Independence area. Not having to pay for shipping probably helped to reduce the prices for these new wagons. It seems that the Murphy type wagons came to dominate the trade, and thus, in a sense, replaced the Pittsburg type wagons on the Santa Fe Trail. The Murphy wagons had deep, flat beds, with straight or only slighted raked box ends, and usually eight bows. (See photo section for a comparison of wagons.) Once the practice of using tandem wagons for freighting developed after the Civil War, it was necessary to have flat beds with straight headboard and tailgates. Often the rear wagon was smaller than the first wagon.

As the trade developed, merchants quickly saw the advantage of having the ability to haul more goods to Santa Fe. William Becknell's first trip was with pack mules. His second trip included not only pack mules, but also three farm wagons loaded with goods. Soon traders wanted bigger and stronger wagons. In 1824, Meredith M. Marmaduke's caravan included two "Road Wagons" and twenty "Dearborns." The Road Wagons had a twelve foot bed, three-and-a-half foot width, and one-and-a-half foot box depth and carried about 1,000 lbs. The Dearborns were much smaller and could carry about 500 lbs. Joseph Murphy opened up his wagon shop in St. Louis in 1841 and built high quality wagons using the best seasoned woods and contruction techniques. By the mid-1840s, his wagons became the standard by which others were judged. Later, a typical Murphy wagon had a sixteen foot bed, was six feet from bottom of the bed to the top of the hoop, eight inch wide wheels, and had seven foot rear wheels. They carried loads between 3,000-8,000 lbs., with loads averaging about 5,000 lbs. Dick Wootton was known to carry up to 10,000 lbs. in some of the wagons he used.

As the wagons became larger so did the width of the wheel rims or iron tires. The rims on small farm and emigrant wagons measured between one-and-three-quarter inches to four inches. The freight wagons had wider wheels. Some of Ben Holladay's largest freight wagons, possibly built by Murphy, had rim widths of ten and twelve inches. The wider wheel width kept the larger and heavier loaded wagons from cutting too deeply into the prairie, and thus, enabling it to roll more easily. While in the early days a six to eight ox team was common, the later larger freight wagons were pulled by ten to twelve ox teams.

Another type of wagon appeared on the trail as the United States military presence grew. By the 1860s, the six mule military wagon, designed to carry supplies and baggage, was in common use, and it continued in widespread use until the late 1870s. Its strength and versatility made it the choice of the U.S. Army, later emigrants, buffalo hunters, and ranchers. The Quartermaster Department specified the wagon to be three feet six inches wide, have a flat box, ten feet long at the bottom and ten feet six inches at the top, with a two inch deep box. A tool box was located at the front and a feed trough at the rear. In some ways it reminded people of the old Conestoga jerkline system with the driver actually riding the mule that was nearest the left front wheel. By the 1870s, a four mule wagon replaced the six mule wagon. It was slightly shorter, narrower, had straight sides and an elliptical spring seat for the driver. These were some of the different wagons associated with the Santa Fe Trail over the years.

Originally, the Mexican authorities were supposed to have placed duties on goods. However, in reality they usually placed the duty not on the amount of goods or size of a wagon, but only on the carrier or on the wagon itself. In 1844, James Webb noted that duties on his goods could have amounted to anywhere from $1,800 to $2,500 per wagon load. Instead, Governor Armijo actually placed a duty of $500 per wagon load. In 1845, the duty per wagon was increased to $950. This practice only served to increase the trader's desire for larger wagons. Traders eager to increase their profits were even known to combine wagon loads and abandon some of their wagons a few days outside of Santa Fe. In 1844, George Bent commented about a Bent caravan noting that its members were headed to Santa Fe with eight wagons but that they " . . . intended to leave two or three before he got to Mora."

People heading west had to decide which type of draft animal to use—horses, mules, or oxen. At the very beginning, horses were used by the trappers and traders, but horses were not practical. The feed requirements for eastern horses were hard to meet along the trail because the best grasses were quickly consumed near the trail. In addition, the Indians preferred horses to mules or oxen, and were more likely to steal them. Within a few years mules and oxen were most commonly used to pull the wagons. They were stronger and had greater endurance than horses. They could survive more easily on the sparce grasses and vegetation along the trail. Oxen were first introduced on the Santa Fe Trail by Major Riley in 1829 and used by Charles Bent in 1830. Thomas Forsyth wrote in 1831 that oxen served three purposes, "1st, drawing the wagon; 2nd, the Indians will not steal them as they would horses and mules; and 3rdly, in case of necessity part of the oxen will answer for provisions." Randolph Marcy in his 1859 guide, *The Prairie Traveler*, took the same position.

Oxen were also cheaper and had larger feet than mules. In 1850, a yoke of oxen (two) cost about $22 and by the 1860s, it cost between $75-$145. Some people held that oxen could survive the bitter cold better than mules could. However, they were more susceptible to sore feet, disease, and did not take the heat as well as mules. While mules were cheaper at first their prices quickly climbed. By 1850 they cost about $200-$400 per span (two), and by the 1860 they cost between $500-$1,000. An article comparing horses and mules appeared in the *1860 Journal Of Commerce*. It noted that mules had a longer working life; their prime was reached when a horse's was starting to decline; mules needed one-third less food to sustain them on the trail; they were less likely to become diseased; and they had a tougher hide. Overall, oxen became the most widely used draft animal on the Santa Fe Trail, then mules, and horses the least used.

A comparison of the different trails can also be made in relation to those who traveled over them. During the first few years of the Oregon and California Trails both sexes traveled the trails. In 1836, Dr. Marcus Whitman and Samuel Parker brought their wives Narcissa Whitman and Eliza Spalding over what later became the Oregon Trail. In 1841, women and children were part of the first party to enter California by way of Oregon. The 1841 Bartleson-Bidwell party, considered to be the first party over the California Trail, also included families. Nancy Kelsey and her baby Ann became the first Anglo-woman and child on the California Trail. From that time on whole families including grandparents, aunts, and uncles often traveled together. The "Great Migration" to Oregon in 1843 included about 200 families.

While during most of the history of the Oregon-

California Trails parties were made up of families, there was one period when the travelers were almost entirely males. This was during the gold rush of 1849. Almost all of the goldseekers were males. However, within a short time families were back on the trails heading to California to make their new homes.

During the first twenty-five years of travel along the Santa Fe Trail the Anglo-American travelers were predominantly males. From the beginning, traders and those hired as teamsters were almost exclusively males. Rarely did Anglo-American women and children travel over the trail, except for the wives and children of a very few traders who might have accompanied their husbands. In 1833, Mary Watt Dodson Donoho and her child Mary A. Donoho were the first Anglo-American women over the Santa Fe Trail. Later, others such as Susan Magoffin and Marion Russell accompanied their husbands. After the Mexican War, the number of travelers, including women, on the Santa Fe Trail increased greatly. After the Civil War period, not only did merchants and traders continue to use it, but also emigrant families desiring to settle in the southwest used it.

While very few Anglo-American women traveled on the trail during its early years, Hispanic and Indian women and children were more commonly encountered. Mexican merchants heading east often were accompanied by their wives and their children who sometimes were to be educated in the United States. In the 1840s, Miguel Otero and Jose Gutierrez were sent to St. Louis, and Francisco Chavez and Joaquin and Francisco Perea were sent to schools in New York. Mexican families were also reported to have traveled east to sightsee and shop.

Although many people think that the Santa Fe trade was undertaken only by Anglo-Americans, this is not true. It was extensively used by Mexican traders. While Becknell may have been given the credit for opening the

Santa Fe Trail, the Mexicans used it heavily. Dr. Manuel Escudero was the first recorded Mexican citizen to take wagons east in 1825. By the 1840s, it appears that the Mexicans dominated the trade between Independence and Santa Fe. In 1842, six Mexican traders were reported to be in Pittsburgh with $350,000 to spend on ". . . waggons [sic], harness, & purchasing other articles . . . ." Many Mexicans also had Anglo-American trading partners. Some of the well-known Mexican and Hispanic merchants and families were the Delgado, Chavez and Manzanares, and Mexican Governor Manuel Armijo. If they were not the proprietors, many of the teamsters and bullwackers were Mexicans. Perhaps the reason why their role has not been emphasized is that the Hispanic traders did not keep records of their ventures as much as the Anglo-American traders did. Or, if the records did exist, they were lost or destroyed during the Mexican revolutions and/or Mexican War. However, if one examines the various register rocks and cliffs along the trail one can see that Hispanic names represent a large portion. Another way to substantiate their important role is by the reference to them in the records kept by the Anglo-Americans.

Thus, by an examination of the characteristics, such as age, length, problems, and usage of the trails west, some clear differences among the trails are evident. While there are many basic similarities, the characteristics mainly associated with the Santa Fe Trail appear to be different from those reflected in the other trails. However, the central significance of all the westward trails is that they played major roles in the development and settlement of the west during the nineteenth century.

THE SANTA FE TRAIL
YESTERDAY AND TODAY

Part I
Early History of the Santa Fe Trail

Early History of the Santa Fe Trail

1609 — The town of Santa Fe was founded under the governorship of Pedro de Peratta. The Spanish government established a policy that kept this distant outpost isolated from contact with the British, French, and later with the Americans.

1700s — Numerous French traders found their way into the Spanish territories and to Santa Fe. The Mallett brothers, Paul and Pierre, traveled in 1739, Luis Feuilli and Jean Chapuis in the 1750s, and Pedro Vial in the late 1700s. Vial first traveled from San Antonio in 1786, then from Natchitocha (Louisiana) in 1787, and finally from Santa Fe to St. Louis in 1792.

1804-5 — One year after the Louisiana Purchase, William Morrison, a Kaskaskia merchant sent Baptiste La Lande, a French Creole, to New Mexico to trade. However, once there, LaLande decided to remain and keep the benefits of his benefactor as his own. He remained, and flourished in Santa Fe.

— Another trader, James (Pursley) Purcell, also traveled to Santa Fe after trading with the Kiowas and Comanches. He became infatuated with Santa Fe, and remained. Some say he found gold at the "head of the Platte," but refused to tell the Spanish because the area had just become part of American territory. Forty-five years later Colorado would have its gold rush.

— The name Boonslick Trail was given to the old Indian/trapper trace west from St. Louis to near Petersburg, Missouri. Nathan Boone, son of Daniel Boone, found a saline springs near the

Missouri River. The following year he and his brother, Daniel, began producing salt there. The Boone family owned the area until 1811.

1806-7 — Zebulon Pike was ordered by General Wilkinson, Governor of Louisiana, to explore the Arkansas River area and to return by way of the Red River. His command totalled twenty-one, including himself: two lieutenants, one Wilkinson son, one surgeon, one sergeant, and sixteen privates. At the Rocky Mountains, Pike named one of the taller mountains Pike's Peak and then turned south into Spanish territory. Captured by the Spanish, he was escorted to Santa Fe. He was finally released and returned to the United States in 1807. His narratives were published in 1810. They stimulated the imagination and interest in the Santa Fe trade with reports of adventure, romance, and profit.

1807 — Jacques Clamorgan, a St. Louis trader, is believed to have led a successful trading trip to Santa Fe and Chihauhau. Other reports indicate that Manuel Lisa and Jacques Clamorgan, St. Louis traders, sent Louison Baudoin to trade in Santa Fe.

1808 — Fort Osage was built as a trading post. The site, on a bluff overlooking a bend in the Missouri, was originally mentioned by Lewis and Clark as a natural location for a fort during their historic expedition of the Louisiana Purchase in 1804–6. In 1824 and 1825 Fort Osage served as a jumping-off place for some of the Santa Fe traders. The 1825 survey of the Santa Fe Trail started there, and then, by 1827, Fort Osage was abandoned. Today much of the fort has been reconstructed.

1809-19 — Over the next decade numerous traders ventured into Spanish territories and Santa Fe to trade only to be captured, have their goods confiscated, and serve time in prison. James McLavanhan, Rueben Smith and James Patterson tried in 1809; Robert McKnight, James Baird, Samuel Chambers and seven others traveled there in 1812. McKnight's party used Pike's report as a guide just as many of the early emigrants to Oregon and California had used Fremont's report. McKnight's party, like the others, was captured and imprisoned by the Spanish.

— In 1817, Auguste P. Chouteau and Jules De Mun traveled to Santa Fe, were captured, had their goods confiscated, and were held by Mexican authorities, but later were allowed to return home. Earlier, Chouteau's party had taken refuge on a heavily wooded island on the Arkansas where they were attacked by Pawnee Indians. Thereafter, the island they had taken refuge on was known as Chouteau's Island. Today the river has changed its course and the island no longer exists. The island also marked the site of the Upper (Cimarron) Crossing of the Arkansas.

— David Merriwether became the last American trader on record to suffer a similar fate. He was captured by Colonel Vizcarra and imprisoned by Melgares. Later in 1853, Merriwether would be named Governor of the Territory of New Mexico.

1817 — The town of Franklin was established on the north bank of the Missouri 205 miles up the Missouri from St. Louis near the end of the Boonslick Trail. Soon it became a boom town. By 1821 steamboats were stopping there. Some reports talked of it surpassing St. Louis, but in 1828, the town and its 1,600 residents were flooded out and Franklin slid into the river. By then other towns were established upriver, and it never resumed its former position of importance.

1821 — Missouri entered the union as a state. Thomas Hart Benton became one of its Senators.

— Mexican Independence was declared on September 27. The joy of independence from Spain brought a brief era of welcome for American traders. However, soon the new Mexican government had the same fears that the earlier Spanish rulers had—too much contact with the Americans would tie Santa Fe to the United States instead of to Mexico.

— William Becknell's mule pack train left from Franklin along the Boonslick Trail and rendez-voused at Arrow Rock. Originally Becknell planned to trade with the Indians. However, after hearing of Mexico's independence, his plans changed. On November 13, Mexican troops approached and urged him to travel to Santa Fe. The route he followed was later known as the Mountain Route. He arrived in Santa Fe on November 16, traded, and then started his return journey to Franklin in December. He returned safely on January 29, 1822, having taken only forty-eight days. Becknell's trip had everyone talking. H. H. Harris, speaking of Becknell's return, is quoted as saying: "My father saw them unload when they returned, and when the rawhide packages of silver dollars were dumped on the sidewalk, one of the men cut the thongs and the money spilled out and clinking on the stone pavement, rolled into the gutter." Becknell had become the "Father of the Santa Fe Trail." Another trader, Thomas James arrived in Santa Fe two weeks after Becknell but did not enjoy the same degree of success and recognition.

1822 — The Santa Fe trade was now underway. Becknell's second expedition of twenty-one members and three wagons left Arrow Rock with $3,000 worth of goods on May 22. From his 1821 experience with his mule pack train, he knew he would not be able to take his wagons over Raton Pass, so instead he cut southwest across the Jornada with his wagons to the Cimarron. He returned from Santa Fe and reportedly made a 2,000% profit.

— Other traders also headed for Santa Fe. Colonel Benjamin Cooper, James Baird, and Samuel Chambers led a caravan which got caught in a snowstorm. They were forced to "cache" or hide their goods in the bank of the Arkansas. In 1823 they returned to get their goods. The holes left after retrieving the goods gave rise to the name "The Chaches" for that area of the Santa Fe Trail. It is located just west of present-day Dodge City, near the Cimarron Crossing.

1823 — Stephen Cooper led the only caravan. He had traveled with his uncle the year before. He took only pack animals, no wagons, and returned with four hundred jacks, jennies, and mules. This was the beginning of the now world-famous Missouri Mules.

1824 — John McKnight, the leader of a party intending to trade with the Indians, was killed. This was the first death associated with the Santa Fe Trail.

— Trade was now well organized. Eighty-one traders, 156 horses and mules, and twenty-five wagons including two carts, two stout road wagons, one field piece, and twenty-one Dearborn Carriages headed southwest to Santa Fe. Traders included Augustus Storrs and Meredith M. Marmaduke, who became, respectively, the American Consul to Santa Fe and the Governor of Missouri. Later, both also wrote accounts of the trail. With an investment of about $30–$35,000, the traders returned with $180,000 in goods and furs.

1825 — The nature of the trail began to change.

— For the most part the Santa Fe Trail was marked and few traders were getting lost. One hundred thirty men made the trip. Ninety were proprietors and only forty were traveling for wages. By 1843, only one of eleven travelers were proprietors.

— Thomas Hart Benton, one of Missouri's first Senators, became spokesperson for the frontier and dreamed of an America "from sea to shining sea." The bill calling for a survey of the road to New Mexican territory and Santa Fe was signed into law by President Monroe shortly before he left office. Congress appropriated $30,000, including $10,000 to survey and mark the route to Santa Fe.

— George Chaplin Sibley, one of three commissioners selected, headed the survey. Joseph C. Brown was named surveyor. Also working in the party were Joseph Reddeford Walker and Benjamin Majors. Walker later became a famous mountain man and guide, and Majors was the father of Alexander Majors, the famous freighter of the Santa Fe Trail. The party left Franklin on

July 4 and moved to Fort Osage which was used as Milepost Zero. On July 17 they set out from Fort Osage. They marked the trail with mounds of dirt. None survives today. The expedition stopped at the Mexican border and finally was given permission to examine, but not mark the route in Mexican lands. Taos, not Santa Fe, was the official Mexican port of entry so the route was surveyed first to Taos and then to Santa Fe. Their report was not submitted until 1827. Unlike Fremont's and Pike's reports about the Oregon and California routes, the notes and maps were not made available to the public. However, they did focus national attention on the trail.

— On August 10, "Council Grove" took its name when the Santa Fe Survey Commission signed a treaty with the Osage Indians in an oak grove on the Neosho River. Sibley had a suitable oak selected in which "to record this name in Strong and durable characters . . ." Shortly thereafter, another treaty was also signed with the Kansa or Kaw Indians at Dry Turkey Creek for safe passage for the traders. However, no treaty was ever signed with the Pawnees, Comanches, Kiowas, Cheyennes, or Apaches which were to prove to be more troublesome.

— The first U.S. Consulate was opened in Santa Fe with Augustas Stores heading it. Mexico opened a consulate in St. Louis, Missouri.

1826 — Two major caravans headed for Santa Fe. One left in May, and the second in August. A seventeen-year-old runaway apprentice named Christopher "Kit" Carson joined the second caravan to Santa Fe. This was the start of his long and famous career as a trader, scout, mountain man, guide, and soldier.

1827 — Cantonment Leavenworth was founded on the bluffs of the west bank of the Missouri. Although this fort was located considerably north of the Santa Fe Trail, it was to be the major starting point for the military presence on the Santa Fe Trail and later for the Oregon and California Trails.

— Independence, Missouri was founded. It was famous for its woods and springs. It soon replaced Fort Osage as the major jumping-off place for the Santa Fe Trail. Courthouse Square would mark the beginning of the trail for the next two decades.

— George C. Sibley was sent to review the route of the Santa Fe Trail in Missouri and Kansas. He renamed Jones' Spring, "The Diamond of the Plains" and Diamond Spring received its new name.

1828 — The town of Arrow Rock was formally platted on the bluffs overlooking the Missouri by Meredith M. Marmaduke, Santa Fe trader and County Surveyor. The town was originally called "New Philadelphia," but citizens referred to it by its commonly-used place name of Arrow Rock. In 1833, its name was officially changed to Arrow Rock by the state legislature. A ferry had been established there in 1811, and it remained in operation until 1927. According to one account, it was Henry Becknell who ferried his brother William across on his way to Santa Fe in 1821. George Sibley had built a fort and trading post there in 1813, but in 1814 he was forced to abandon it because of increased Indian trouble.

— Two Franklin traders, Daniel Monroe (Munroe) and the son of Samuel G. McNees (first name unknown) were returning from Santa Fe. They rode ahead of the party. They stopped to rest at a stream, were found asleep by Comanches, and were shot with their own guns. When the rest of the party reached them, it was too late. McNees was dead. The stream and crossing at which he was killed came to be called McNee's Creek and Crossing. The wounded Monroe was carried on to the Cimarron where he died and was buried. During the funeral service a small band of Indians, perhaps Pawnees, approached. The angry traders killed all but one of them who returned to his camp. A few days later the Indians attacked the traders and stole nearly 1,000 head of horses and mules.

— The Comanches attacked the next Santa Fe party which included twenty-five people with four or five wagons and 150 mules. Captain John Means was killed. The other traders in the caravan were finally forced to abandon their property and were barely able to make it back to Missouri alive. Their arrival back home increased the cry for protection for traders.

— Six traders had now been killed. Three had been killed in 1828 and three had been killed between 1821 and 1827.

1829 — As mule stealing by Indians increased, the first reported use of oxen by traders was made. The military had used oxen the year before.

— Council Grove had now developed into the organizational point for the traders. Here they formed larger caravans and performed their final checks before venturing further west into the more hostile plains.

— President Andrew Jackson authorized U.S. Army protection for the Santa Fe traders. Major Bennett Riley from Fort Leavenworth led four companies of the Sixth Infantry to escort the traders to the international border with Mexico at Chouteau's Island where he set up camp. The traders proceeded into Mexican territory. The traders were surprised by a party of Kiowas and a fight ensued. Mr. Lamme, an owner of the caravan was killed. A messenger was sent to Major Riley who brought his troops to rescue the caravan. The Kiowas left, but Major Riley continued on some forty miles to Sand Creek and then returned to the border. This was probably the first time such a large armed American force entered Mexican territory.

— Riley remained in the area until October. Mexican Colonel Antonio Viscarra escorted the traders back to the Arkansas. While on their return trip, the traders appeared to take out their revenge for the previous spring's killing of Lamme by fighting Arapahoes and Comanches along the way. Upon the meeting of the two forces at Chouteau's Island, the Americans and Mexicans hosted each other with a celebration and feast. On October 14, the two groups headed back to their respective areas—Riley to Missouri and Viscarra to Santa Fe.

1831 — Jedediah Smith, the famous mountain man and explorer, was killed by Comanches near the Cimarron River. He was part of the Smith, Fitzpatrick, Jackson, and Sublette caravan of twenty-five wagons and eighty men. While crossing the dreaded Jornada they ran into trouble. Smith went ahead to locate water, found a buffalo trail and followed it. At a dry riverbed he scooped out some sand and found water. Some Comanches came upon him and a fight ensued. Smith was killed along with two Comanches.

— The nature of the trail began to change. Tourists began to arrive. The volume of trade began to increase dramatically. Wagons were larger and business was conducted on a much larger scale. Trade began to continue through Santa Fe further south to Chihuahua, and by 1840 half of all trade continued south.

1832 — George and Robert Bent brought the first wagons north over Raton Pass.

1833 — Westport was founded by Isaac McCoy a few miles west of Independence. With the later development of Westport Landing in what is now Kansas City, Westport became another major starting point along the Santa Fe Trail. By 1843, it was the eastern terminus of the Santa Fe Trail.

— Charles and William Bent and Ceran St. Vrain built a trading post, "Fort William" on the Arkansas River. However, to the traders it was commonly referred to as Bent's Fort. From 1833 until 1849, this fort served as the major resting point for all who traveled the Mountain Branch of the Santa Fe Trail. It also served as a major military rendezvous location during the Mexican War in 1846. In many respects the role of this fort was similar to that of Fort Laramie on the California and Oregon Trails. Fort Laramie on the

Oregon-California Trail was also originally called Fort William, but became known by its common name, Fort Laramie. Even today, both Fort Laramie and Bent's Fort are major attractions for tourists along the two major trails.

— There was a wet spring along part of the Santa Fe Trail. Because of the heavy rains the wagons taking Cimarron Cutoff across the Jornada cut a clear and deep path for all who followed in later years.

1834 — The spring caravan of eighty wagons and 160 men, including sixty proprietors was captained by Josiah Gregg and later by Ira Smith, brother of Jedediah Smith. Captain Clifton Wharton and Company A of the Dragoons from Fort Gibson served as an escort for traders along the Santa Fe Trail to the crossing of the Arkansas. This was the first mounted escort for traders. The 1829 caravan had been escorted by foot soldiers. For much of the trail the Pawnees and Comanches followed the caravan, but they finally left after the army and traders crossed the Arkansas. The army then returned and Captain Wharton later reported that he did not think troops were needed in the eastern section between Walnut Creek and the Arkansas because the Indians were friendly. During the fall return the caravan traders reported no Indian trouble.

1838-9 — In Santa Fe the import duty was raised to $500 a wagon. Yankee traders counteracted by using larger wagons that could haul more goods.

1836-43 — Relations between the Texans and Mexicans worsened during the years after Texas became independent. By 1841 tensions and emotions were at a peak. Texans went to raid the Mexican caravans and to seize control of Santa Fe. On September 17, 1841, the Texan Santa Fe Expedition was forced to surrender to Mexican Governor Manuel Armijo's army. George Wilkins Kendall, an American journalist with the Texan Santa Fe Expedition, was one of the captured. His book, *Narrative Of The Texan-Santa Fe Expedition*, published in 1844, would become the *Uncle Tom's Cabin* of the Mexican War. In it was the description of the great suffering the Texan captives experienced while in the hands of the Mexicans as they were forced to march to Mexico City and then held captive until April, 1842.

— In 1843, "Captain" John McDaniel, claiming to have been recruited by "Texan Colonel" Warfield, held up the Don Antonio Jose Chavez's caravan near present-day Lyons, Kansas and killed Chavez. His body was thrown into a creek ravine which today bears a corrupt form of Chavez's name, Jarvis Creek. Relations worsened with America because Mexico feared U.S. ties with Texas. In 1843, Jacob Snively raided Mexican caravans along the Cimarron Cutoff and forced the Mexican government to close down trade in northern Mexico in August. The American Captain Philip St. George Cooke disarmed and disbanded the Texans. The Mexican order to close down trade was later rescinded on March 31, 1844, but it was too late for a spring caravan to form.

1844 — Josiah Gregg's two volume *Commerce Of The Prairies* was published about the Santa Fe Trail and trade. The reviews were great, and it became a classic handbook for anyone interested in the Santa Fe area and trade.

1846 — This was the year that changed the history of Santa Fe. War was declared on Mexico on May 13. After the war, trade was no longer an international concern.

— Although political relations between Mexico and the United States were strained, commerce along the trail seemed more normal. Traders were arriving in Independence on a regular basis. The early spring Santa Fe caravans of Speyer and Webb left Independence before war was declared and arrived in Santa Fe on June 30. While the Mexicans knew war had been declared, they still escorted the traders to Santa Fe, and they in turn paid the duty of $625 per wagon. It seemed as though it was business as usual. Shortly, however, Santa Fe was to feel the impact of the war as the U.S. Army used the Santa Fe Trail as its invasion route during the summer months.

— The later spring caravan rendezvoused at Council Grove on June 19 & 20 with the knowledge that war had been declared. Samuel Magoffin's train and his new bride, Susan, were members of this caravan. Susan wrote her now famous diary, later published as *Down The Santa Fe Trail And Into New Mexico* on this trip. Her diary includes information about the delays the traders experienced because of the war. It also describes the rumors and news the traders heard concerning the war while on the trail.

— General Stephen Kearny commanded the Army of the West, including the Mormon Battalion under Philip St. George Cooke, which marked down the Santa Fe Trail. The various companies and all their supplies jammed the trail and held up normal traffic all along the way, including trade at Bent's Fort. Army supply trains were leaving for the west nearly every three or four days. James Magoffin, Samuel Magoffin's brother, accompanied Captain Cooke's advance party into Santa Fe and is said to have made it possible for Kearny to enter Santa Fe without bloodshed. Kearny entered Santa Fe on August 18 without a fight, and Santa Fe was now an American town. Lt. Emory laid out the site for Fort Marcy on a hill overlooking Santa Fe. From Santa Fe, Kearny and later the Mormon Battalion would head west to California.

— Relations between the Americans, Mexicans, and Indians began to worsen during the Mexican War. As more Americans came to Santa Fe conditions deteriorated.

— Monthly stage service between Fort Leavenworth and Santa Fe became regular. The trip took nearly four weeks and cost $150. Conditions for passengers along the way were spartan at best. Not until the 1860s did conditions for stage passengers become more comfortable as stage stations or stops were developed along the trail.

1847 — On January 19, an Indian uprising in Taos resulted in the death of seven people including Charles Bent who was serving as the first Governor of New Mexico. By February 4, General Price had cornered and defeated most of the insurgent Indians in Taos, but Indian trouble occurred all along the trail and even at Bent's Fort.

— The army constructed a new fort, Fort Mann, about halfway between Fort Leavenworth and

Santa Fe. It was located near the Caches by present day Dodge City. It was to provide protection from Indians along the trail, but it was abandoned within a short time.

— The various Indian tribes now realized that their way of life was coming to an end as wagon after wagon came through their lands. Conditions were reported to have gotten so bad that it was even suggested that all of New Mexico be bought from the private owners and returned to the Indians.

1848 — While the fighting between the Americans and Mexicans had ended in early 1847, the formal Treaty of Guadalupe Hildago was not signed until February 2, ending the Mexican War. The United States territory now included the present-day states of New Mexico, Arizona, Utah, Nevada, and California. The Santa Fe Trail was now completely and officially within American territory.

— Professional freighting was on the rise. Alexander Majors started freighting. He left Independence, Missouri on August 10 with six wagons and teams. He made the round trip in ninety-two days with the same oxen. He later joined with Russell and Waddell. By 1856, they had 350 wagons, and by 1858, 3,500 wagons, 4–5,000 men, 40,000 oxen and 1,000 mules. However, not all these were engaged in the Santa Fe trade. Many of them were used in freighting on the other western trails. Other people took up freighting as the need for goods and supplies increased due to the permanent and growing civilian and military presence in the Southwest.

— An early winter settled upon the plains. Many companies reported the loss of stock. Even the

Missouri River froze over at Independence. Southwest of Bent's Fort, Lt. E. F. Beale reported that one man and ninety mules froze one night.

1849 — The California gold rush started. Thousands of men, wagons, and animals were crowding the jumping-off spots for the journey west. Independence was one of these. While most gold seekers took the Oregon-California Trail, estimates range from a low of 2,500 to a high of 8,000 gold seekers who took the Santa Fe Trail to Santa Fe. However, all who left from Independence followed the Santa Fe Trail until the Oregon-California Trail branched off. Most of those who decided to take the Santa Fe Trail followed it to Santa Fe and then followed either the Old Spanish Trail or the Gila River Route into California. Some of the gold seekers had gone earlier to California with General Kearny in 1846. Also coming with the increase in emigration on the trail was the dreaded disease cholera.

— On August 20–21, William Bent, depressed over the loss of his brother Charles and the decline in his business, abandoned and partially destroyed his old fort. Later, William built a new fort further east near Big Timber.

— James M. White and his family were returning to Santa Fe from Independence. He, his wife (Ann), daughter (Virginia), and a black slave rode ahead of the caravan. Near Point of Rocks they were surrounded by Jicarilla Apaches under Chief White Wolf, and a fight ensued. Mrs. White and her daughter were taken captive and the others were killed. After the wagon train caught up, a messenger was sent to Santa Fe for help. Later

Captain Grier and a company of dragoons with Kit Carson as scout pursued the Indians and caught them. Instead of attacking, Grier paused to talk. The Indians became aroused and fighting broke out. When it was over, Mrs. White was found shot by the Indians, but nothing was ever found of the child. Many of the Indians escaped.

1850 — One of the major tragedies of the trail happened. Sometime around May 12 a mail coach with ten men was attacked by Apaches and Utes at Wagon Mound. All ten men were killed.

— July 1 marked the start of regular monthly mail service between Independence and Santa Fe. David Waldo, Jacob Hall, and William McCoy, all of Independence, Missouri, were partners in the venture and were given the mail contract for four years. At first there was only one stage a month leaving each way on the first of the month. Within a few years, passenger stages were regularly making the trip. They started out once a month, twice a month by 1857, once a week in 1858, and three times a week in 1866, and later daily. In addition to carrying the mail there was room for eight to eleven passengers, depending on the coach. Stage stations were needed along the trail and the land between them was being tamed. The charge for the trip was originally $250, then $200, and by 1857, $150 in winter and $125 in summer months.

— Bertram Spratt drove the first scheduled mail stage. He left Independence on July 1, and arrived in Santa Fe on July 28. He started his return trip on August 1 and arrived in Independence on August 28.

— Freighting with the Army continued to increase and become big business as more and more contracts were signed. On September 4, Brown, Russell & Co. contracted for goods weighing over 600,000 pounds. Within a month, four wagon trains of thirty wagons and one of fifteen set out. David Waldo also got into the freighting business when he signed a contract with the Army to freight their supplies from Fort Leavenworth to Santa Fe. Within the month two different trains of thirty wagons each were also off to Santa Fe.

— Fort Atkinson was established by Colonel Sumner near the earlier location of now abandoned Fort Mann. Atkinson was a sod fort and was briefly called Fort MacKay. It became the major fort near the lower Arkansas Crossing and the only fort along the central portion of the trail. It was abandoned in 1854, much to the dismay of the Santa Fe traders.

1851 — Fort Union was constructed. It was situated near the junction of the Mountain Branch and the Cimarron Cutoff. There were three forts constructed at this spot. The first, a log fort in 1851, the second, an earthen Star Fort in 1861 during the Civil War, and the third and final adobe fort was built from 1863–69. This last fort was finally closed on February 21, 1891. While Fort Union was first constructed to protect the commerce along the trail, it also served as a depot for the other smaller satellite forts that were activated in the southwest to protect not only the Santa Fe Trail, but also the growing settlements in other parts of the southwest.

1852 — William Bent moved his trading operation down to Big Timbers and completed his large stone fort in 1853. This was Bent's New Fort. However, Indian trade as he knew it was coming to an end. Unable to sell it, he finally leased the fort to the U.S. Army in 1860, and it was used as part of the army's New Fort Wise.

1853 — Thomas Fitzpatrick, U.S. Commissioner, signed a peace and friendship treaty for the United States with the Kiowas, Comanches, and Apaches on July 27. It granted the United States the right to establish military forts and railroad depots along the trail. In return it provided for a ten year annual payment of $18,000 worth of goods and provisions to the three tribes. The Indians moved south of the Arkansas. This treaty was the beginning of the end for both the Indians and the Santa Fe Trail. The railroad would ultimately come to replace the Santa Fe Trail and the Indians would be forced from their lands. Further north on the Oregon-California Trail, a similar type of treaty, the Horse Creek or Fort Laramie Treaty, had been signed two years earlier in 1851.

— Fort Riley was built on the Kansas River near the Big Blue. After Fort Atkinson was abandoned, Fort Riley became the new supply depot for the Army.

— "Windwagon" Thomas encouraged the harnessing of the prairie wind and the development of wind-driven wagons to carry the freight on the prairie. After a frightful maiden voyage both his wind-wagon and idea ended in a crash.

— The Diocese of Santa Fe was created under the direction of the Right Reverend J. B. Lamy.

1854 — Another cholera epidemic hit the Central Plains and the Santa Fe Trail. Stories of pain and death spread all along the trail.

— Alexander Majors & William Russell signed contracts to haul government freight. This represented a change from hauling freight for merchants to hauling goods for the government.

1857 — Hockaday and Hall stages now left Independence and Santa Fe on the 1st and 15th of the month. The cost for trips leaving between May 1st and November 1st was $125 and $150 for trips between November and April. The time was estimated to be twenty to twenty-five days. By the 1860s a trip by stage was down to just under two weeks, but the large freight wagons trains still took about three months.

— The Spanish Fever, a bovine disease, spread along the trail and killed many of the oxen.

1858 — Gold was discovered in the Pike's Peak area. Perhaps this was the source of James Pursley's legendary gold. The Santa Fe Trail became one of the three major routes to the Colorado Rockies. One route followed the Oregon-California Trail leaving it at Julesburg. The second followed the Smoky Hill Trail through central Kansas, and the third followed the old Santa Fe Trail west and then finally left the Mountain Branch to head north.

— Relations with the Indians worsened and travel along the Cimarron Cutoff almost came to a halt. Thieves, other than Indians, were also preying on the traders along the trail.

1859 — The Kansas Legislature approved the Articles of Incorporation for the Atchison & Topeka Railroad with Cyrus K. Holliday as founder. In 1863, after the Land Grant Bill became law, the railroad was directed to build "in the direction of Fort Union and Santa Fe, New Mexico." The railroad changed its name to the Atchison, Topeka, and Santa Fe. It was given ten years to reach the Colorado State Line.

— Fort Larned was established in October. At first it was called "Camp on Pawnee Fork" and later Camp Alert. It was in the heart of the Indian buffalo hunting grounds. It played a major role in handling the Indian hostilities of the 1860s in the Central Plains. By the mid-1860s the old sod and adobe buildings were being replaced by the stone buildings which are still standing. The last major role played by the fort was to protect the crews who were building the railroad that soon replaced the Santa Fe Trail. The fort was abandoned in 1878.

1860 — Fort Lyon was established in August by Major John Sedgwick near Bent's New Fort. It was originally named Fort Wise after the Governor of Virginia. However, with the advent of the Civil War, the fort's name was changed. After Governor Henry Wise joined the Confederacy the fort was named after Union Brigidier General Nathaniel Lyon. Then it functioned as the post protecting traffic from Confederate incursions into the Central Plains and from increased hostilities by the Indians in the Central Plans and along the Mountain Branch. One of Fort Lyon's less than noble roles was when it served as the base of operations for Colonel John Chivington and the Colorado Volunteers. It was from here that they perpetrated the infamous massacre of Chief Black Kettle's peaceful band of Cheyenne at Sand Creek.

1861 — Kansas became a state and entered the Union and Colorado became a territory.

1862 — The Civil War brought more danger to the Santa Fe Trail. The Army had to protect the trail not only from the increased Indian attacks, but also from guerilla raiders and the threat of the Confederate Army. From Westport to Diamond Springs, Confederate guerillas took a heavy toll. Many stage stations along the trail were attacked. The Cimarron Cutoff was nearly abandoned. The mail route was changed to the Mountain Branch and remained so even after the end of the Civil War. In 1863, a Santa Fe trader named Wilson, his wife, and family were killed near McNee's Crossing.

— In July of 1861, Fort Union's massive earthen Star Fort was begun. It was completed in June of 1862. While one officer at first announced the fort to be almost impregnable, later another officer showed that it was wide-open to attack from the brow of the mesa to its west. Fortunately, the fort never saw action against the Confederates.

— The Confederate Army invaded New Mexico from the south along the Rio Grande. In February, Union Colonel E. R. S. Canby was defeated by General H. H. Sibley at Valverde, and he withdrew to Fort Union and was ordered to hold it. Sibley and his Confederate Army captured Albuquerque and Santa Fe. Now only Fort Union was left to be captured.

— The most famous Civil War battle in the West was fought between March 26–28 at Glorieta (Martin) Pass and in Apache Canyon as the Confederates marched towards Fort Union. Fighting occurred on the Santa Fe Trail near the Pigeon's and Johnson's Ranches. Confederate Major Charles L. Pyron and Colonel William R. Scurry were defeated in a series of battles led by Union officers Major John Chivington and Colonel John P. Slough. The Confederates withdrew to Santa Fe and then, with the advance of General James H. Carleton with 2,350 men, the Confederates withdrew from New Mexico completely. After that, only the Indians were a problem for the Santa Fe travelers.

1864 — Two additional forts, Fort Zarah and Fort Dodge, were laid out on the Santa Fe Trail. Fort Zarah was located on Walnut Creek, near Great Bend. It was named after General R. S. Curtis' son who was killed by Quantrill's Raiders. Escorts were provided for traders between Fort Larned in the west and Council Grove in the east. The fort was abandoned in 1869 after most of the Indian trouble ended.

— Fort Dodge was located near the Cimarron Crossings of the Arkansas. It played a major role during the Indian campaigns that began during the end of the Civil War. The fort even came under attack by the Comanches and Kiowas in September of 1868, as did the traders along the trail. The fort served as General Sheridan's base of operations in 1868-69 during his successful campaign against the Indians of the southern plains. The fort was abandoned in 1882, and it is now a state soldiers' home.

1865 — Fort Larned's sod and adobe structures were replaced by sandstone block structures. The first structure completed was the blockhouse on February 20, 1865. Most of the other stone structures were completed by 1868.

— In May, Colonel Kit Carson, upon orders from General James Carleton, established Camp Nichols in Oklahoma territory on the Cimarron Cutoff. It was to act as a "desert halfway station . . . between Fort Union and the Cimarron Crossing of the Arkansas." It provided escorts along the cutoff. By fall the stone fort was abandoned, but it had successfully served its mission that summer. This was the fort described by Marion Russell in the book, *Land Of Enchantment.*

— George C. McBride and Richens Lacy "Uncle Dick" Wootton built a toll road over Raton Pass with bridges and improved roads. They received a charter from Colorado and New Mexico to build the twenty-seven mile road. They even blasted away the infamous Devil's Rock, an overhanging rock which forced traders right to the edge of the trail. The toll was one dollar and fifty cents a wagon; one dollar for a smaller vehicle; twenty-five cents for horsemen; and five cents per head of stock. Indians traveled free. At his stage stop, meals were seventy-five cents and board fifty cents. It was reported that Wootton would throw the toll into an empty whiskey keg until it was filled. Then, he would take it to Trinidad and put it in the bank. McBride kept the ledger and in a little more than a year he reported $9,193.64.

— The period after the end of the Civil War saw another great change which finally brought an end to the Santa Fe Trail: the construction of the railroad.

— The Kansas Pacific began at Wyandotte, opposite Kansas City in 1863 and began to push west toward Denver. As it did, the eastern terminus of the Santa Fe Trail moved westward with the westernmost tip of the railroad. In 1865 the railroad was at Lawrence, in 1866 at Topeka, and by 1867, at Hays City.

— William Cody was hired by the Kansas-Pacific to hunt buffalo to feed its hungry work crews. Earlier he had hunted buffalo with "Buffalo Bill" Mathewson at his Cow Creek store. However, to the Kansas Pacific crews Cody became "Buffalo Bill."

1869 — Kit Carson, the trader, mountain man, scout and soldier who grew up with the Santa Fe Trail, died.

1868-78 — The railroads continued to move westward. In 1869, the railroad was at Sheridan, and by 1869–70 it was at Kit Carson, Colorado. In 1873, a spur was run to West Las Animas near Bent's Fort. As the Kansas-Pacific moved west, traffic along the Cimarron Cutoff almost came to a halt.

— In 1868, the Atchison, Topeka, and Santa Fe Railroad finally broke ground in Topeka; by 1870, it was at Emporia; by 1871, it was at Newton; and in 1872, it was first at Great Bend, then Dodge City, then finally at the state line. By the end of 1875, it was at La Junta and in 1878, at Trinidad.

1879 — Two railroads wanted the route over the Raton Pass, but Wootten had granted the Atchison, Topeka, and Santa Fe Railroad the right to use his toll road over the Pass. The railroad zigzagged its way up the mountain. On July 14, a tunnel was completed through the mountain. With its completion, Dick Wootton's toll road finally came to an end on September 9, 1879.

1880 — The headlines of Santa Fe's newspaper *New*

Mexican, read "The Old Santa Fe Trail Passes into Oblivion." The first train rolled into Santa Fe on February 16, and with that the old Santa Fe Trail—the road of commerce—came to an end. While some local traffic followed parts of the trail, the grand old highway leading from Missouri to the land of adventure, profits, and romance was no more.

— There is one interesting story to add. By 1879 the Atchison, Topeka, and Santa Fe Railroad had decided not to complete the line the last thirty miles northwest into Santa Fe. Instead the railroad was to turn southwest to Albuquerque and then to head towards California and the Pacific. The citizens of Santa Fe became incensed and sold bonds to finance the construction of the railroad the final thirty miles to Santa Fe. With their success, the Santa Fe Trail came to an end.

Part II
Maps—Guides—Diaries

Maps—Guides—Diaries

Editor's Note:
The diary excerpts have been reproduced with original spelling and phrasing in order to present an authentic picture of the times.

VERY FEW GOOD maps of the Santa Fe Trail were available to travelers during its early years. However, just before and during the time of the Mexican War, as U.S. military activity increased in the area, so did the mapping of the area and the Santa Fe Trail.

Four good items which pre-date the Mexican War period are included. The first two items are part of the 1825 Sibley Commission's Survey of the Santa Fe Trail. Joseph C. Brown was the chief surveyor. Included are the portions of Brown's notebook that show the route along the Arkansas River from near the Little Arkansas approaching the Great Bend down along the Arkansas River to the area of The Caches. These sections also correspond to the following diary section. The second item is the 1827 map of the trail based on the Sibley Commission and Brown's Survey. The map was very good, but, unfortunately, neither the notebook nor the map were available for the travelers because it was never published. The third item indicating part of the Santa Fe Trail is the "Map of the Western Territory &c." It was published in 1834 for the 23rd Congress and identifies the road as the "Waggon Road to St. Louis" or as the "Santa Fe Road." A decade later, and probably the first widely published map to show the whole Santa Fe Trail was Josiah Gregg's, "A Map of the Indian Territory Northern Texas and New Mexico," published in 1844 in his popular *Commerce Of The Prairies*.

From the Mexican War period come two maps showing the trail. One, Fremont's "New Mexico and the Southern Rocky Mountains," was compiled by Lieutenant J. W. Abert with Lieutenant W. G. Peck's assistance in 1845. At this time, Lieutenant Abert was serving with Captain Fremont who was exploring the western regions. This was the best map of the plains. A year later in 1846–7, Lieutenant Abert and Lieutenant Peck under Lieutenant William Emory continued the mapping of the Santa Fe Trail. Lieutenant Emory was in charge of the mapping of the route as General Kearny's Army of the West invaded Mexico, took Santa Fe in 1846, and moved on to California. Although Kearny's army started at Fort Leavenworth, they soon joined the mainline of the Santa Fe Trail and followed it to Santa Fe via the Mountain Branch. Fremont's map is reproduced and part of Emory's map which also includes the works of Abert and Peck is shown.

BROWN'S NOTEBOOK PAGES
National Archives

These pages are from Joseph Brown's notebook showing part of the route that corresponds to the trail route described later in the diary section. Note that although the writing is meant to be read from left to right, the trail is shown from the east to the west. Therefore, south is on the top and north at the bottom.

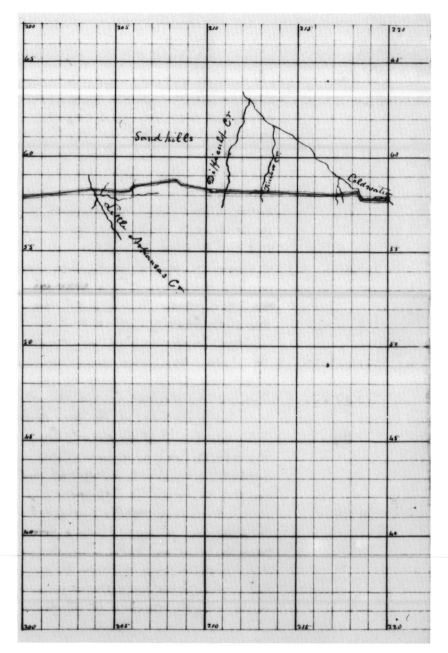

230.07 5 17 6 6 At the crossing of the little Arkansas there is wood for fuel & the water & grass are tolerably good; having crossed the Creek travel up a a small

7 48 Creek of it—Continuing on the South side of it, there is no timber on this Creek which is short, when at the head of it—the Sand hills will appear a few miles to the left.

237 55 5 10 18 Difficult Creek 15 links runs South-ward into Cold water there is no timber near the road on it, & the bed is ra-

2 . ther soft & bad to cross.

239 55 5 08 18 Timbered C.k 10 d. runs South? it should be crossed just at the upper timber

7 09 water & grass tolerably good.

246 44 5 01 09 Cold Water or Cow Creek is a nar-row stream from 30 to 50 links wide, for the most part miry, banks com-monly high; there is tolerable cross

15 56 ing just above the largest body of timber on it, which is very conspicuous; on the two branches East? of the creek is timber. The camp ing is good on this Creek for wood water grass &(commonly) Buffalo

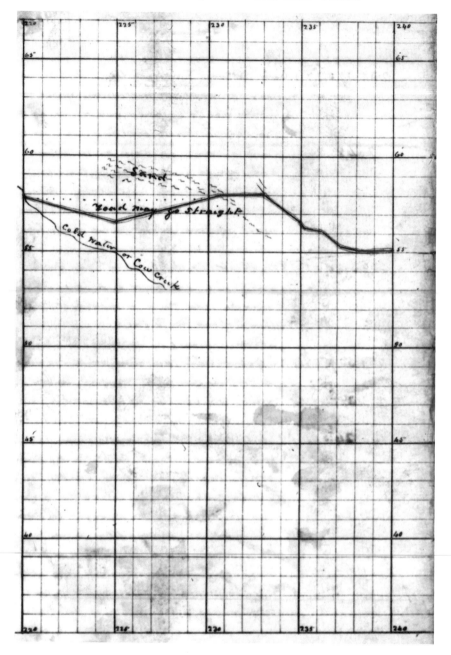

From Cow Creek the traveller should
be careful not to bear too much to
the left or he will get on the sandy,
he may travel directly west or as
little north of west as he may
262.40 485 33 choose to fall on the Arkansas,—
After crossing Cow Creek, the
beaten road which hitherto has
been plain, will probably be
seen no more as a guide; The
Arkansas will be the guide for
about two hundred miles, In
general the travellers should not
keep near the river as tis sandy—
Near the foot of the hills the ground
is firm & the travelling better, Where
it is necessary to turn in to the
river to camp tis commonly best
to turn in short— or at right
angles, & fuel may be picked
up almost any where, & there
10 01. grass is commonly pretty
good, Generally the river is a
quarter of a mile broad & may be
crossed on horse back almost
any where if the banks permit &
they are generally low, The water
is pleasant in this part of the
river & above.

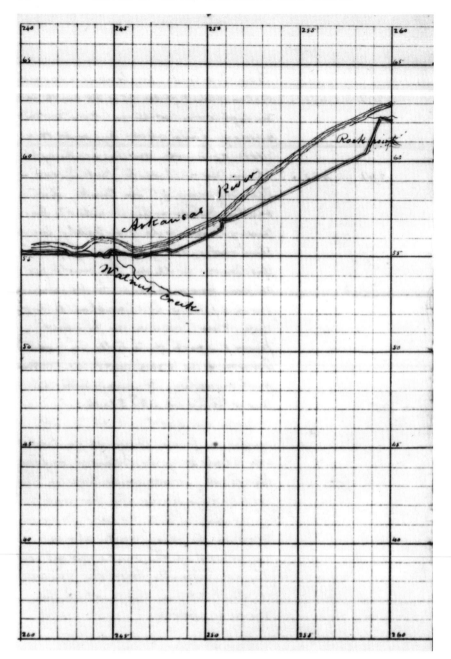

272	41	475	32	Walnut Creek from 60 to 160 links wide runs into the Arkansas at the North bend a little above a handsome grove of timber on the South part of the river called "Pit-Grove" The Crossing of the Creek is directly between the bends of the river next below & next above the Creek, The ford is good. On this Creek is more timber than
	25	24		on any from Council grove principally low crooked ash & elm, when in Season plenty of plums are to be had here & the Camping is very good for water fuel & grass, The latitude of this place is 38° 21′ 10″
				The road may continue straight By Rock point as dotted to the crossing of the Creek above it.

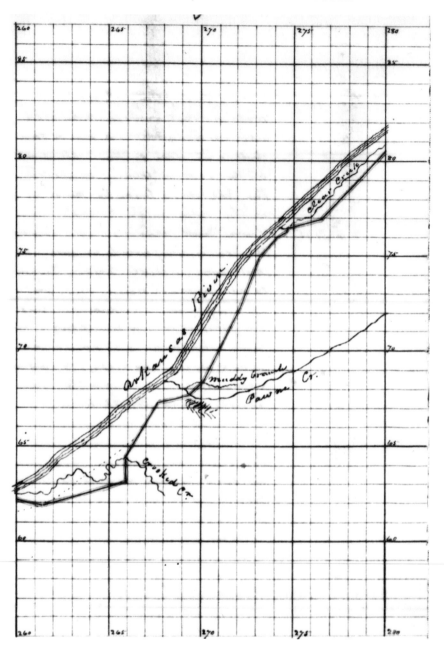

297	65	450	08	Crooked Creek 5t Links wide bears S.E. & affords plenty of excellent wood & grass but the water is not very good. Its bed is shaded with Ash & Elm. It may be crossed in many places. In the fall it is nearly dry.
	4	61		
302	40	445	27	Pawne Creek 100 Links wide runs nearly East, ford tolerably good west bank a little soft. The ford is at the South point of a sort of bluff. The Camping is good for grass & water & tolerable for fuel the Creek is shaded with Elm & ash. From this point Some travellers prefer to continue up on the South Side of this Creek for some distance, then Crossing it Several times. Continue westward passing the head waters over to the Arkansas, as being nearer than the river but the river route is more safe & convenient for man & beast.
	10	77		
313	43	434	30	Mouth of Clear Creek a small stream of transparent run.

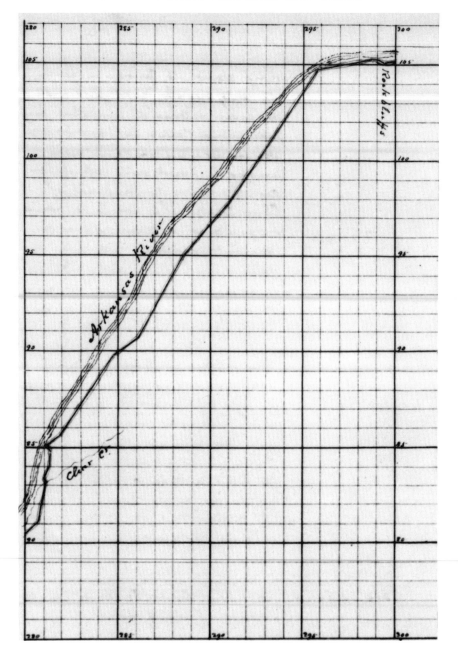

41 19

ning water: its Course is from its head, nearly parralled with the river & near it, in what may perhaps be Called the river bottom. On the South Side of the river among the sand hills which border it opposite the head of Clear Creek, Elk are to be found & a few deer, & when in Season plums & grapes —

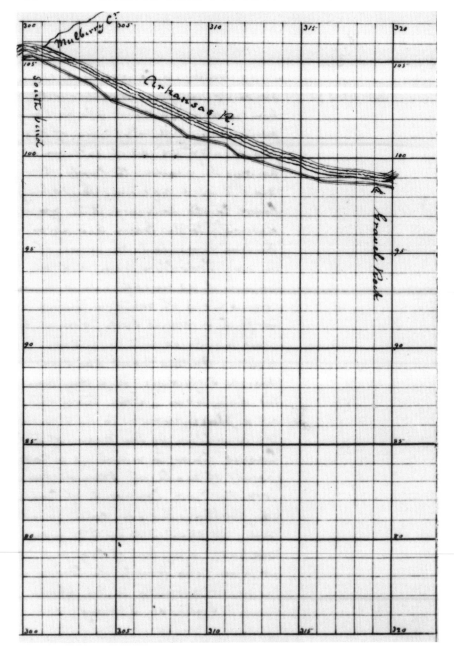

| 354 | 62 | 393 | 11 |

South Bend of the Arkansas R. here is the first rock bluff seen on the river. the latitude of this place is 37° 38'. 52" . It would be much nearer to cross the river here & ascend Mulberry Creek to its source & then go directly to the lower spring on the Semaron, but on trial of the way Travellers have discontinued it as unsafe. It is incommodious of water & timber for fuel, & wants such prominent land marks as will be a sure guide. On this rout has been much suffering; in a dry time tis dangerous — Some turn off at a place known to the Santa Fe Travellers by the name of the "Cashes" near to which is a rocky point of a hill at some distance from the river Composed of Cemented pebbles, & therefore called gravel rock. At about 3 miles S.W. from this rock is a place of Crossing for those who travel the lower rout, or directly to the afore named Semaron Spring; but

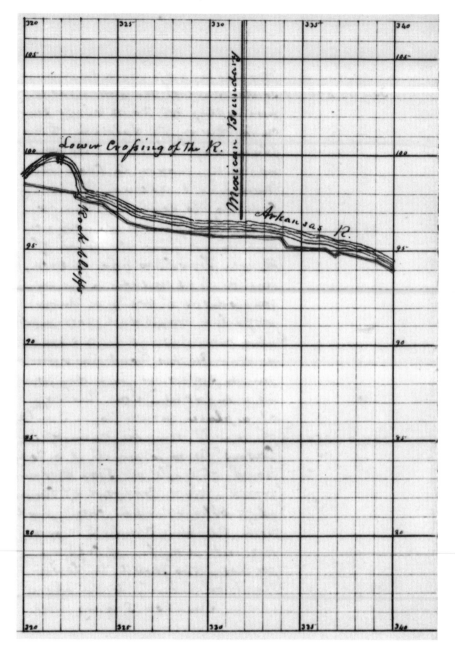

this (tho in a less degree) is subject to the same objections as that directly from the South bend. The road this way is good & in the spring, & early summer, to those who may be acquainted with it, or may have a compass to direct them, it is about 30 miles nigh-

33 22

er than the upper route. The direct Course from this point to the spring is S 71¾ W 71 miles. But the upper route is more safe for herding stock & more commodious to the traveller, as he will always be sure of wood & water on the river, & a sure guide, & in general it is easier to kill Buffalo for provisions —

388 04 359 69 The Mexican Boundary or 100th degree of Longitude West from Greenwich is where a few Cottonwood trees stand on the North Side of the river about 1½ miles above a timbered bottom on the same side. At this timbered bottom is very good Camping for grass & fuel.

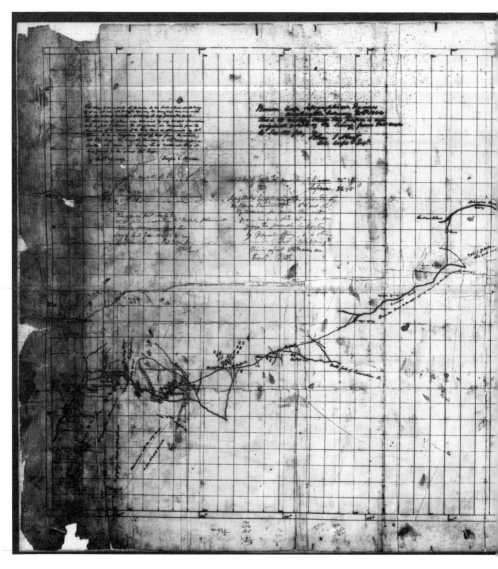

BROWN'S MAP
National Archives

This map was originally drawn with a scale of one inch to twelve miles. However, a larger set of two sections was made with a scale of one inch to four miles. If all Brown's materials had been available to the public, perhaps American history would have been different.

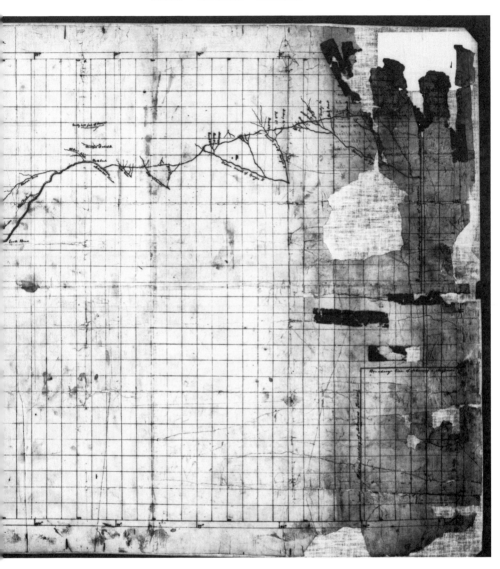

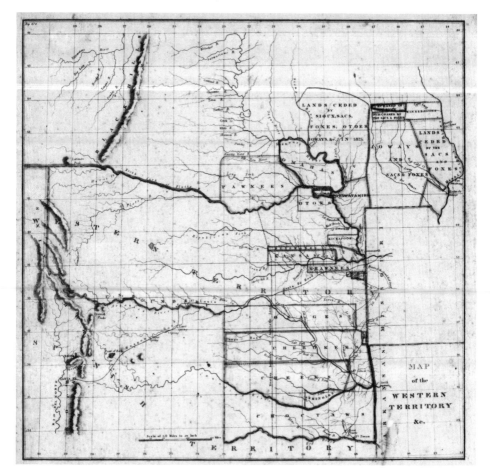

MAP OF THE WESTERN TERRITORY
National Archives

This is one of the earliest maps of the trail published for Congress in 1834. Its overall size was small and had a scale of one inch to fifty miles. It is especially interesting because it shows the Cimarron River feeding into the Arkansas and not feeding the North Fork of the Canadian River. This indicates the lack of adequate knowledge of the area between the Arkansas and the Canadian River and especially of the area called the Jornada of the Cimarron Cutoff.

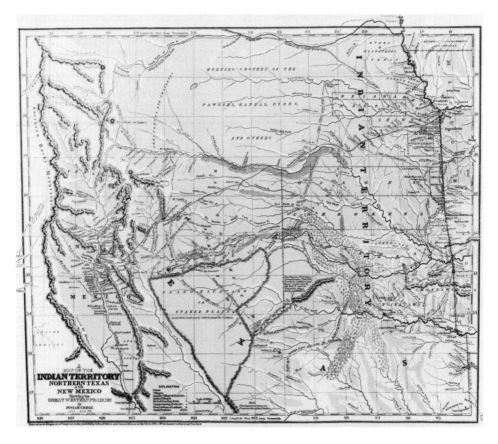

GREGG'S MAP
Commerce Of The Prairie

This was the first readily available map indicating the route of the Santa Fe Trail. It was published in his popular two volume book, *Commerce Of The Prairie*. Note the differences in the river locations with the preceeding 1834 map. This shows the increased geographical knowledge of the west and Santa Fe Trail just prior to the Mexican War.

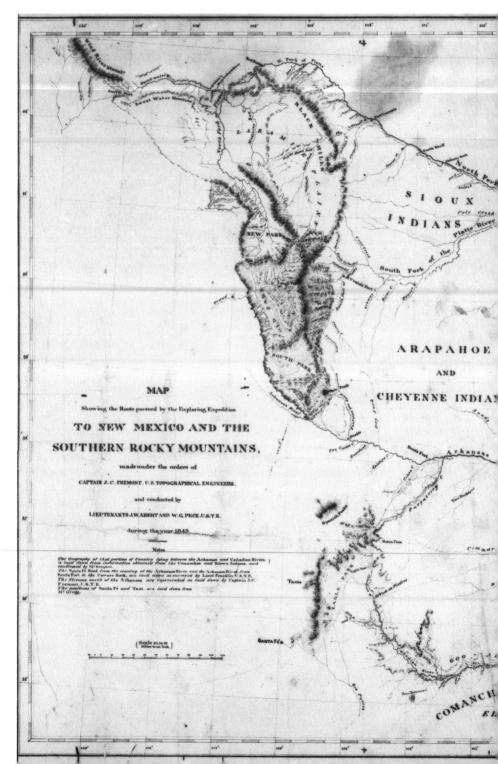

MAP

Showing the Route pursued by the Exploring Expedition

TO NEW MEXICO AND THE

SOUTHERN ROCKY MOUNTAINS,

made under the orders of

CAPTAIN J. C. FREMONT, U.S. TOPOGRAPHICAL ENGINEERS,

and conducted by

LIEUTENANTS J.W. ABERT AND W.G. PECK, U.S.T.E.

during the year 1845

Notes

The Geography of that portion of Country lying between the Arkansas and Canadian Rivers, is laid down from information obtained from the Comanche and Kiowa Indians, and confirmed by Mr Simpson.
The Santa Fe Road from the crossing of the Arkansas River, and the Arkansas River from Bents Fort to the Pawnee Rock, are laid down as surveyed by Lieut Franklin, U.S.T.E.
The Streams north of the Arkansas are represented as laid down by Captain J.C. Fremont, U.S.T.E.
The positions of Santa Fe and Taos, are laid down from Mr Gregg.

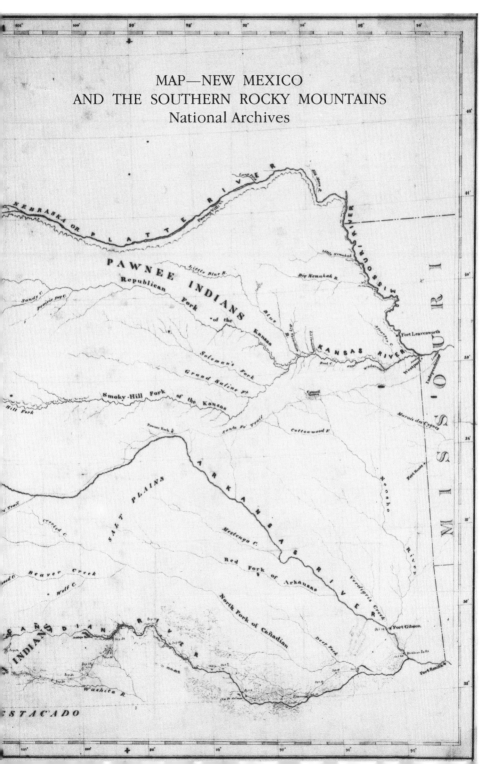

MAP—NEW MEXICO
AND THE SOUTHERN ROCKY MOUNTAINS
National Archives

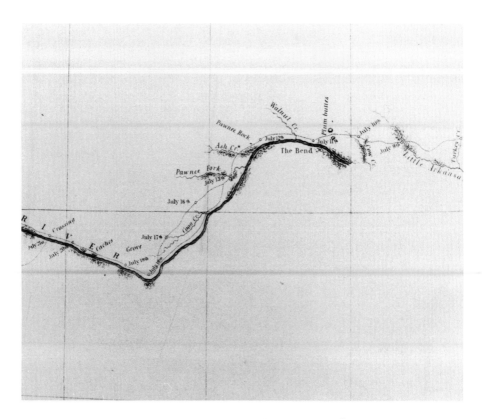

LIEUTENANT EMORY'S MAP, 1847
National Archives

This portion of Emory's map corresponds to the area described in the diary section from Cow Creek to the Great Bend down along the Arkansas to The Caches.

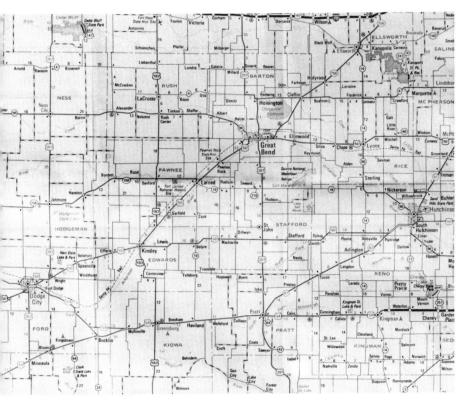

OFFICIAL KANSAS HIGHWAY MAP

This recent road map of Kansas is the identical area covered in Emory's map of 1846.

When studying the different trails west one of the interesting aspects to investigate is the occurrence and use of guidebooks. However, what is discovered is the general lack of trail guides regarding the Santa Fe Trail, especially during its first forty years. Yet, for the Oregon and California Trails numerous guidebooks of varying quality appeared on the scene within a couple of years of the opening of those trails. Lansford Hastings, Joseph Ware, Hosea Horn, Andrew Child, and Franklin Street produced guidebooks for California and/or Oregon, but none were produced for the Santa Fe Trail. How can this be accounted for?

The answer appears to lie in the history and nature of the trails themselves. The nature of travel over the Santa Fe Trail during its sixty year period from 1820 to 1880 was different from travel over the two other famous trails west, the Oregon and California Trails. As discussed earlier, the main use of the Santa Fe Trail was for commerce or the transportation of goods. In a sense, the people came along with the goods. However, the other two main trails were developed to bring people to new territories to start new lives, and the goods came along with or after the emigrants.

The guidebooks were largely produced for the use by emigrants who would travel perhaps only once over a trail in their lifetime. The emigrants were not knowledgeable about the area to which they were traveling. They were farmers, shop owners, doctors, and women with children. They were largely unfamiliar with extended periods of travel over new lands with varying terrain and unfamiliar dangers. For them, a good trail guide was almost a necessity. Some of the earliest Oregon and California emigrants realized this and decided that they might profit a little from their own journeys. Therefore, they kept very good diaries which were the bases for their guidebooks which they printed within a year or two after their journey.

However, most of those who traveled the Santa Fe Trail during its early years were trappers, traders, and entrepreneurs. They traveled the trail many times. Their guidebooks were etched into their minds and could be recalled as required. Their livelihood depended on their knowledge and it was too important to keep in a small book or on pieces of paper that could be lost in the wind or ruined in a stream crossing. They did not plan on making a profit from a guide about the trail, but from their own travel over the trail. Yet, maps and guides slowly became available.

The earliest written guide and record of the trail was produced by the U.S. government. It was based on the survey of the trail made by the Sibley party in 1825. It included information about mileage, water, grass, stream crossings, etc. This survey could have become an extremely valuable guide, but unfortunately, it was never published or made available to those nineteenth century travelers or to the general public. It seems to have been put away and almost forgotten. As a matter of fact, it was first published in 1952, one hundred twenty-five years after it was compiled. It has only been in recent years that the Sibley-Brown Survey has received its rightful attention. (See the map section for copies of part of the survey.)

One of the entrepreneurs who did publish about his experiences on the trail was Josiah Gregg. While his work was not published as a guidebook, it easily served the same purpose. His two volumes included information about a variety of topics, all of interest to those who would travel and trade in the Southwest. It included material about: the historical development of the trail; preparations for travel; the routes; organizing a caravan; the geography of the area; the Mexican and Indian inhabitants; customs of the peoples; animals—wild and domestic; Mexican government; Mexican industries; and many other topics. His table of mileage, camping, and landmarks is included. His map of the trail is also reproduced along with other maps in the map section.

Another of the few journals which was also intended for use as a guide was Edward Beale's *Central Route To The Pacific* which included part of the Santa Fe Trail. It was published in 1854. It started in Westport and followed

* Having crossed the Prairies between Independence and Santa Fé six times, I can now present a table of the most notable camping sites, and their respective intermediate distances, with approximate accuracy—which may prove acceptable to some future travellers. The whole distance has been variously estimated at from 750 to 800 miles, yet I feel confident that the aggregate here presented is very nearly the true distance.

From INDEPENDENCE to	M.	Agg.		M.	Agg.
Round Grove,	35		Sand Cr. (leav. Ark. r,)	50	442
Narrows,	30	65	Cimarron r.(Lower sp.)	8	450
110-mile Creek,	35	100	Middle spr. (up Cim. r.)	36	486
Bridge Cr.,	8	108	Willow Bar,	26	512
Big John Spring,			Upper Spring,	18	530
(crossing sev'l Crs.)	40	148	Cold spr. (leav.Cim. r.)	5	535
Council Grove,	2	150	M'Nees's Cr.,	25	560
Diamond Spring,	15	165	Rabbit-ear Cr.,	20	580
Lost Spring,	15	180	Round Mound,	8	588
Cottonwood Cr.,	12	192	Rock Creek,	8	596
Turkey Cr.,	25	217	Point of Rocks,	19	615
Little Arkansas,	17	234	Rio Colorado,	20	635
Cow Creek,	20	254	Ocatè,	6	641
Arkansas River,	16	270	Santa Clara Spr.,	21	662
Walnut Cr.(up Ark. r.)	8	278	Rio Mora,	22	684
Ash Creek,	19	297	Rio Gallinas (Vegas),	20	704
Pawnee Fork,	6	303	Ojo de Bernal (spr.),	17	721
Coon Creek,	33	336	San Miguel,	6	727
Caches,	36	372	Pecos village,	23	750
Ford of Arkansas,	20	392	SANTA FE,	25	775
27					

the Santa Fe Trail west into present-day Colorado. But since Beale's goal was Los Angeles, California, and not Santa Fe, it did not continue down to Santa Fe. Instead, after leaving Bent's Fort, it continued to Fort Massachusetts and then over Coochatope Pass, on into Utah, and then along the Old Spanish Trail into California. The itinerary for the Santa Fe portion is included.

One guidebook that did include a mile by mile

ITINERARY OF THE CENTRAL ROUTE.

From Westport, Missouri, to Los Angeles, California.

DATE.	CAMPS.	DIST-ANCE.	DISTANCE FROM W.	REMARKS.
May 15	Ind. Creek		12	Cottonwoods, willows, good grass.
" 16	Bull Creek	23	35	Some timber; good grass and water.
" 16	Garfish Creek	22	57	Nearest wood, half mile; water and grass.
" 17	"110"	23	80	Running stream; timber, good grass.
" 17	Dragoon Creek	12	92	" fine timber and grass.
" 18	Stream	10	102	Good water; timber and grass.
" 18	"	4	106	" " "
" 18	Hollow	6	112	Water in holes; grass.
" 18	COUNCIL GROVE	10	122	Settlement; abundant timber; grass; water.
" 19	Hollow	17	139	Water; grass and timber abundant.
" 19	Lost Spring	15	154	Good water, not abundant; grass; no wood.
" 20	Cottonwood Creek	16	170	Large timber; running water; good pasturage.
" 20	Turkey Creek	19	189	Plenty of water and grass; no wood.
" 21	Pool	12	201	Grass and water; small bushes.
" 21	Little Arkansas	18	219	Good timber; grass and water.
" 21	Owl Creek	10	229	Timber and grass; no water, except after rains.
" 22	Great Bend of Ark.	35	264	Wood; grass and water.
" 22	Walnut Creek	7	271	" "
" 23	Pawnee Fork	31	302	Well wooded; grass and water.
" 23	Pond	9	311	Good pasturage; water; no wood; plenty "buffalo chips."
" 24	"	25	836	Water; grass.
" 24	Arkansas River	20	356	Water; grass; small bushes.
" 25	FORT ATKINSON	5	361	" " "
" 26	1st Crossing of S. Fé trail	10	871	" " "
" 26	2d " "	5	876	" " "
" 26	Camp on Ark.	20	396	" " "
" 27	"	20	416	" coarse grass; no wood.
" 28	Island on Ark.	19	435	" " little wood.
" 28	Chouteau's Island	12	447	" coarse rank grass; drift-wood.
" 29	Slough of Ark.	28	475	" wiry grass; no wood.
" 29	Arkansas River	8	483	" " "
" 30	Big Timbers	20	503	" coarse grass; large timber.
" 30	Arkansas River	12	515	Good water; abundant bottom grass; timber.
" 31	Lower Dry Creek	25	540	Scanty dry grass; water in pools, warm; wood.
" 31	BENT'S FORT	7	547	Bottom grass; river Arkansas; wood.
" 31	Upper Dry Creek	7	554	" " "
" 31	Pond	6	560	Dry bunch grass; water; wood near river.

approach to the Santa Fe Trail was Randolph Marcy's *The Prairie Traveler: A Handbook Of Overland Expeditions*, written in 1859. The War Department asked him to write it specifically for emigrants. The Santa Fe Trail is described in only two small parts in his "List of Itineraries." One, "II. From Fort Leavenworth to Santa Fe, by way of the upper ferry of the Kansas River and Cimarron," and the second, "XVII. From Westport, Missouri to the gold diggins at Pike's Peak and 'Cherry Creek,' N.T., via the Arkansas River." As noted, the first one starts at Fort Leavenworth and the other one from Westport. The former follows the Santa Fe Trail across the Jornada on the Cimarron Cutoff to Santa Fe, while the latter one continues along the Arkansas and then follows what was part of the Mountain Route. This section is similar to Beale's itinerary. However, Marcy's continues to Pike's Peak and does not turn southwest to cross the Raton Mountains. Both of Marcy's itinerary sections are included here. Although both sections cover much of the same route, the mileages listed and the items recorded differ slightly.

The parts that corresponds to the diary sections are from Fort Leavenworth, "Miles 18.19. Little Arkansas River" to "Miles. 25.34. Lower Crossing of the Arkansas." and for the guide section from Westport, "Miles. 23. Little Arkansas River." to about "Miles. 18¾. Arkansas River." Most of Marcy's book dealt with the basic information needed by emigrants. It included advice on a variety of areas: California and Oregon, organization of wagons, packing, camping, fording, foods, animals, Indians, hunting, and others. All of this was helpful for the emigrants.

Diaries written by travelers along the Santa Fe Trail appear to be scarcer than those written by travelers along the Oregon and California Trails. The majority of the people who traveled along the Santa Fe Trail were

260   FORT LEAVENWORTH TO SANTA FÉ.

Miles.

cedar, and is firm and good. Camp is in sight of the town of Questa, upon a very elevated bluff.

21¾. Laguna Colorado.—Road passes through a wooded country for a portion of the distance, but leaves it before reaching camp, where there is no wood, but water generally sufficient for trains. In very dry seasons it has been known to fail. The road forks here, the right leading to Santa Fé *via* Galistio (45½ miles), and the left to Albuquerque.

22½. San Antonio.—Good road.

18¾. Albuquerque.—Good road.

Total distance from Fort Smith to Albuquerque, 814¾ miles.
Total distance from Fort Smith to Santa Fé, 819 miles.

II.—*From Fort Leavenworth to Santa Fé, by the way of the upper ferry of the Kansas River and the Cimarron.*

[In this table the distances, taken by an odometer, are given in miles and hundredths of a mile. The *measured* distances between the crossing of the Arkansas and Santa Fé are from Major Kendrick's published table. Wood, water, and grass are found at all points where the absence of them is not stated.]

Miles.

From Fort Leavenworth to

2.88. Salt Creek.

9.59. Stranger's Creek.

13.54.   "

9.60. Grasshopper Creek.

6.50.   "

2.86.   "

2.60.   "

4.54. Soldier's Creek.

2.45. Upper Ferry, Kansas River.

7.41. Pottawatomie Settlement.

5.75. Pottawatomie Creek.

3.89. White Wakarussi Creek.

7.78.   "   "

6.27.   "   "

0.73. Road from Independence.—No place to encamp.

5.72. White Wakarussi Creek.

Miles.

2.51. White Wakarussi Creek.

2.82. 142-mile Creek.

7.80. Bluff Creek.

5.77. Rock Creek.

5.08. Big John Spring.

2.29. Council Grove.

7.97. Elm Creek.—Water generally.

8.06. Diamond Spring.

1.42. Diamond Creek.

15.46. Lost Spring.—No wood.

9.25. Mud Creek.—Water uncertain; no wood.

7.76. Cottonwood Creek.

6.16. Water Holes.—Water generally; no wood.

12.44. Big Turkey Creek.—No water.

7.83. Little Turkey Creek.—Water uncertain; no wood.

18.19. Little Arkansas River.

10.60. Owl Creek.—Water generally in holes above and below crossing.

6.39. Little Cow Creek.—Water only occasionally.

2.93. Big Cow Creek.—Water holes, 10 miles (estimated).
Water uncertain; no wood.

18.24. Bend of the Arkansas.

6.66. Walnut Creek.

16.35. Pawnee Rock.—Teams sometimes camp near here, and
drive stock to the Arkansas to water. No wood.

5.28. Ash Creek.—Water above and below crossing, uncertain.

6.65. Pawnee Fork.—Best grass some distance above crossing.
From Pawnee Fork to the lower crossing of the Arkansas, a distance of 98½ miles, convenient camping-
places can be found along the Arkansas; the most
prominent localities are therefore only mentioned.
A supply of fuel should be laid in at Pawnee Fork to
last till you pass Fort Mann, though it may be obtained, but inconveniently, from the *opposite* side of
the Arkansas. Dry Route branches off at 3½ miles
(estimated). This route joins the main one again 10
miles this side of Fort Mann. It is said to be a good
one, but deficient in water and without wood.

11.43. Coon Creek.

46.58. Jackson's Island.

5.01. Dry Route comes in.

262   FORT LEAVENWORTH TO SANTA FÉ.

Miles.
10.05. Fort Mann.
25.34. Lower Crossing of the Arkansas.—The Bent's Fort
Route branches off at this point. For the distances
upon this route, see next table. A supply of wood
should be got from this vicinity to last till you reach
Cedar Creek.
15.68. Water-hole.—Water uncertain; no wood.
30.02. Two Water-holes.—Water uncertain; no wood.
14.14. Lower Cimarron Springs.—No wood.
20.00. Pools of Water.—Water uncertain; no wood.
19.02. Middle Springs of the Cimarron.—No wood.
12.93. Little Crossing of the Cimarron.—No wood.
14.10. Upper Cimarron Springs.—No wood. Pools of water,
7 miles (estimated). No wood.
19.05. Cold Spring.—A tree here and there in the vicinity.
Pools of water, 11 miles (estimated). Water uncertain; no wood.
16.13. Cedar Creek.—M'Nees' Creek, 10 miles (estimated).
Water indifferent and uncertain; scant pasture; no
wood. Arroyo del la Seña, 2½ miles (estimated).
No water.
21.99. Cottonwood Creek.—No water. Arroyo del Burro, 5
miles (estimated).
15.17. Rabbit-ear Creek. — 10 miles (estimated), springs.
Round Mound, 8 miles (estimated). No water; no
wood; no camping-place. Rock Creek, 10 miles
(estimated). Grazing scant; no wood.
26.40. Whetstone Creek.—Spring; no wood. Arroyo Don
Carlos, 10½ miles (estimated). Water, etc., to the
left of the road.
14.13. Point of Rocks.—Water and grass *up the cañon*, just
after crossing the *point;* scattering shrub cedars on
the neighboring heights.
16.62. Sandy Arroyo.—Water uncertain; no wood. Crossing
of Canadian River, 4¼ miles (estimated). Grazing
above the crossing; willows.
10.05. Rio Ocaté.—Wood ⅓ of a mile to right of road; grass
in the cañon. Pond of water, 13½ miles (estimated).
No wood.
19.65. Wagon Mound.—Santa Clara Springs. Wood brought
from the Rio Ocaté. Rio del Perro (Rock Creek),
17½ miles (estimated).
21.62. Cañon del Lobo.—Rio Moro, 3½ miles (estimated).

Miles.

    Rio Sapillo, 1 mile (estimated).   The Bent's Fort
    Route comes in here.
18.00. Las Vegas.—Forage purchasable.
13.05. Tacolote.—Forage purchasable.   Ojo Vernal, 5 miles
    (estimated).   No grass to speak of.
14.00. San Miguel.—Forage purchasable; no grass.
21.81. Ruins of Pecos.—Grazing very scant.   Cottonwood
    Creek, 4½ miles (estimated).   Water uncertain; no
    grass.
13.41. Stone Corral.—No grass.
10.80. Santa Fé.—Forage purchasable; no grazing.

III.—*Camping-places upon a road discovered and marked out from Fort Smith, Arkansas, to Doña Aña and El Paso, New Mexico, in 1849.* By Captain R. B. MARCY, U. S. A.

Miles.

    Fort Smith to
65. South Fork of the Canadian.—The road from Fort
    Smith to the South Fork of the Canadian follows the
    same track as the road to Albuquerque and Santa
    Fé, and by reference to the tables of distances for that
    road the intermediate camps will be found.
15. Prior's Store.—Grass, wood, and water near.
17¼. Little Boggy.—Good camp.   Wherever there are not
    the requisites of wood, water, and grass for encamp-
    ing, it will be specially noted; when they are not
    mentioned they will always be found.
13. Little Boggy.—Good camp.
15½. Boggy Depôt.—Store and blacksmith's shop.
12¾. Blue River.—The road passes over a flat section, which
    is muddy after rains.
8½. Fort Washita.—Good camp half a mile before reaching
    the fort.   The road forks at the Indian village on the
    Boggy, the left being the most direct.   There are set-
    tlers along the road, who will give all necessary in-
    formation to strangers.   Corn plenty.
22. Preston Texas, on Red River.—The road from Fort

Miles.
10.40. El Paso.—Well at El Paso supplying 100 animals;
    water muddy and brackish; grass poor.
52.00. Sonorita.—No water on the road; at Sonorita are sev-
    eral brackish springs. Grass poor; bad camping-
    place; saltpetre at the springs.
    Quita Oaquita.—No water on the road. Saline spring
    at camp, better than at Sonorita, but the grass is not
    so good.
10.40. Agua Salado.—Water uncertain; grass poor.
23.40. Los Pleyes.—Water only in the rainy season, one mile
    west of the road, hidden by bushes and difficult to
    find. Grass pretty good.
28.60. Cabeza Prieta.—Natural tenajas in a ravine two miles
    from the road; follow a wagon-track up this ravine
    between a black and a red mountain. The water is
    good and abundant; grass tolerable.
31.00. Poso.—No water on the road until reaching Poso.
    Here it is abundant on the east side of the road;
    grass good one mile west.
13.00. Rio Gila.—But little good grass.
26.00. Fort Yuma, at the crossing of the Colorado River.—
    But little good grass for several miles.

Total distance from El Paso to Fort Yuma, 756 miles.

XVII.—*From Westport, Missouri, to the gold dig-*
gings at Pike's Peak and "Cherry Creek," N.
T., via the Arkansas River.

Miles.
    Westport to
4¾. Indian Creek.—The road runs over a beautiful country.
    Indian Creek is a small wooded stream, with abund-
    ance of grass and water.
8¾. Cedar Creek.—The road passes over a fine country, and
    there is a good camping-place at Cedar Creek.
8½. Bull Creek.—The road is smooth and level, with less
    wood than before. Camping good.
9½. Willow Springs.—At nine miles the road passes "Black
    Jack Creek," where there is a good camping-place.
    The road has but little wood upon it at first, but it in-

Miles.

creases toward the end of the march. The road is level for some distance, but becomes more rolling, and the country is covered with the finest grass. Good camp at one mile from the main road.

20¼. 110-Mile Creek.—The road traverses the same character of country as yesterday, but with less woodland, is very smooth, and at 9 and 12 miles passes "Rock Creeks," which have no running water in a dry season. Good camp.

22½. Prairie Chicken Creek.—At eight miles the road crosses Dwissler Creek, which is a fine little stream; four miles farther First Dragoon Creek, and at one mile farther the Second Dragoon Creek, both fine streams, well wooded, and good camping-places. Good camp.

20. "Big Rock Creek."—At one mile the road crosses a small wooded branch. Three miles beyond it crosses "Elm Creek," where a good camping-place may be found. At 7 miles it crosses 142-Mile Creek, and at 13 miles it crosses Bluff Creek, where there is a good camping-place. Good camp.

20. "Council Grove," on "Elm Creek.—Road passes "Big John Spring" at 13 miles, and is smooth and good. A fine camp is found three fourths of a mile beyond the "Grove," on Elm Creek, with abundance of wood, water, and grass.

16. Diamond Spring.—At·eight miles the road crosses Elm Creek, and passes over a section similar to that east of Council Grove. It is fine in dry weather, but muddy after heavy rains. Good camp at Diamond Spring.

16. Lost Spring.—One mile from camp the road passes a wooded creek. From thence there is no more wood or permanent water until arriving at camp. Take wood here for cooking, as there is not a tree or bush in sight from Lost Spring. The country becomes more level, with grass every where. The road is muddy in wet weather.

15¾. Cottonwood Creek.—Road continues over a prairie country, sensibly rising and improving. Wood, water, and grass at camp.

22. Turkey Creek.—The road is good, and at 18 miles passes Little Turkey Creek. No wood, and the water poor at camp; grass good.

23. Little Arkansas River.—The road runs over a level prai-

298 WESTPORT TO PIKE'S PEAK.

Miles.

rie, and at 3½ miles passes "Big Turkey Creek," with the Arkansas River Valley in sight all day. After rains there are frequent pools of water along the road. Good camp.

20. "Big Cow" Creek.—The road passes for ten miles over a level prairie to Charez Creek, which is a bushy gully; thence six miles to Little Cow Creek, which is a brushy stream, with here and there a tree. Good camp here to the left of the road, near a clump of trees. "Prairie-dog towns" commence to be seen. Road very level. Buffalo-grass here.

20. Big Bend of the Arkansas.—The road at 12 miles strikes the sand-hills of the Arkansas River. They are soon passed, however, and the level river bottom is reached. The river has a rapid current flowing over a quicksand bed. The road is generally good from the last camp. Wood, water, and grass at camp.

7. Walnut Creek.—The road is good. Cool springs at this camp; good grass and wood.

21. Head of Coon Creek.—At five miles the road forks, one following the river, the other a "short cut" "dry route" to Fort Atkinson, where they unite on the river. The country rises for ten miles on the dry route, then descends to the river, and is covered with the short buffalo-grass. No wood at camp.

18. Arkansas River.—The road passes over an undulating and uninteresting prairie, with but little vegetation. The water in dry weather is in pools.

19. Arkansas River, at Fort Atkinson.—The road runs over a similar country to that of yesterday, with no wood near; plenty of buffalo-chips for cooking, and good grass.

18¾. Arkansas River.—At 4½ miles the road ascends a bluff covered with thick buffalo-grass. On the river is heavy bottom-grass. At 17 miles pass a ford. Grass good at camp.

19¼. Arkansas River.—The road is sandy for 14 miles, but not deep except in places; thence to camp it is good. Good camp.

22. Arkansas River.—Country prairie, covered with short buffalo-grass. Good camp.

22. Arkansas River.—The road is fine, crossing several dry beds of creeks, along which are seen a few scattering trees. Good camp on a dry creek near the river.

Miles.

24. Arkansas River.—The road runs over a barren plain at the foot of the main plateau, and crosses two dry creeks near the camp, on which are cottonwood-trees. Plenty of wood at camp.

21. Arkansas River.—The road follows the base of the hills at from one to three miles from the river. Good camp.

20. Arkansas River.—At seven miles the road strikes the "Big Timbers," where there is a large body of cotton-wood; thence for three miles the road is heavy sand. Good camps along here.

13. Arkansas River.—At one mile the road passes some old houses formerly used as a trading-post. Here terminates the "Big Timbers." Coarse grass at the camp.

15. Arkansas River.—At three miles the road passes the mouth of Purgatoire Creek. Camp is below Bent's Fort. Good grass here.

24. Arkansas River.—Pass Bent's Fort. The grass is excellent in the vicinity of the fort, but after this it is not so good. The road runs over a high and considerably broken country. Good camp.

11. Arkansas River.—Opposite the mouth of the Apishpa Creek; good camp. The Huerfano Mountains and Spanish Peaks are in sight from the camp. The "Cherokee Trail" comes in from Arkansas near Bent's Fort, and leads to the gold diggings at Cherry Creek.

9. Arkansas River.—Opposite the mouth of the Huerfano Creek. Good camp, and a ford opposite Charles Audebee's house.

12. Arkansas River.—At this point the Cherokee trail bears to the right and leaves the river. The left-hand, or river road, runs up to the old pueblo at the mouth of the Fontaine qui Bouille Creek. The right-hand road leads to the gold diggings.

15¾. Fontaine qui Bouille.—The road strikes in a northwest course over the rolling country, and comes upon the creek at a most beautiful camp, where there is a great abundance of good wood, water, and grass. The wood, water, and grass are good at all points on the Fontaine qui Bouille, and travelers can camp any where upon this stream.

17½. Fontaine qui Bouille.—Here the road forks, one running up the river, and the other striking directly across to engaged in commerce and usually traveled over it numerous times. Recording their experiences was not a high priority. Also, fewer people traveled over the Santa Fe Trail than the Oregon and California Trails. However, there are a number of printed accounts which are available to those interested in following the trail as the emigrants and traders did more than one hundred years ago.

For historians, these diaries are one of the major sources of insights into the trail's development, the nature of commerce in the southwest, the clash and diffusion of cultures, and the traders and emigrants themselves. Each diary is different, and no single diary can be considered the definitive one. Conditions on the trail could change from day to day, not to mention from one year to the next during the trail's sixty year history. Different sections of the trail had varying characteristics and placed different demands on the travelers. The role of the individual and the reason for travel over the trail—trader, hired hand, emigrant, gold seeker, or coach passenger had an impact on the diary of the person and what each recorded. Even men and women say things differently. Each wrote from his/her own perspective, interest, and expectations. All these factors combined to give each traveler his/her own special reaction to the trail, and thus, it was reflected in the diary and made each diary different from others.

Therefore, each diarist could report different impressions of the trip along the trail. This is not to say that they did not have similar experiences, however. Only by examining a variety of dairies can one better understand the trip west to Santa Fe.

The following diary excerpts are by three different travelers: George Sibley (1825), U.S. survey leader, (Kate Gregg's *The Road To Santa Fe*, University of New Mexico Press); Josiah Gregg (1844), trader; and Susan Magoffin

(1846), bride, (*Down The Santa Fe Trail And Into Mexico*, edited by Stella Drumm, Yale University Press). Each diary has been considered a classic for its own reasons. Although the three excerpts are from different years, each will give some insight into what life on the trail was like. See how their different positions and perspectives influenced their record of the trail. Gregg's and Magoffin's diaries are readily available in bookstores and museums, while Sibley's might be found in some libraries.

By the time the travelers had reached the Arkansas River they had come about 270 miles, give or take twenty miles depending on where they began. For the next few weeks they would follow the valley of the Arkansas River. The worst part of the Santa Fe Trail still faced them—the crossing of the Jornada on the Cimarron Cutoff or the climb over the Raton Mountains on the Mountain Branch.

Come join our three diarists while they were still traveling along a pleasant section of the trail as they met the Arkansas and traveled along it to The Caches. Later, Magoffin would head further west along the Arkansas taking the Mountain Branch, while Sibley and Gregg would cut southwest across the dreaded Jornada to the Cimarron River from near The Caches. Both the Mountain Route and the Cimarron Cutoff finally joined together again in the area where Fort Union was constructed and then all travelers headed for Santa Fe along the same trail.

As you read each diary, note their comments concerning their expectations and fears, the problems met during the different years, and the climatic and physical conditions found and endured.

Two maps that were included earlier correspond to the same areas described in the diary sections. The first is a section of Emory's map published in 1847. It covers the trail from near Cow Creek to the Great Bend on the Arkansas River and then along it to The Caches.

The second, a recent highway map of Kansas, shows the identical area represented in Emory's map of 1847. For those driving in their car, it should be easier to locate the sites described in the diaries.

Read along and relive the diarist's journey as each headed southwest over the Santa Fe Trail along the Arkansas River.

George Sibley was in charge of the party that made the survey of the Santa Fe Trail in 1825. The party used Fort Osage as milepost Zero and their starting point on July 17, 1825. Sibley noted, "The surveyor is instructed to note all the course very exactly, and to measure as he proceeds." In addition to the specifics of the route, Sibley comments on prairie animals encountered. On August 18, they struck the Arkansas and by September 10, were at area of The Caches.

> **Tuesday 16th August.**—The Morning fair & pleasant. The Wind from the South West. After breakfast The Commissioners met the Kansas formally in council. The Treaty was exhibited in due form, containing all the stipulations required by the Act of Congress, and the prompt payment of $800 in full compensation for the right of way through the Territory of the Kansas forever—all of which was read and carefully explained, and then the Parties signed and executed the Treaty in due form, a Duplicate copy of which was given to the Head Chief, after which, we delivered them Goods to the value of Three Hundred Dollars, St. Louis Cost; and gave them an Order on Curtis & Eley, Traders near them, for Goods such as they may want to the value of Five Hundred Dollars, at fair cash prices. The chiefs expressed their perfect satisfaction with this arrangement. While they were dividing their Goods, I wrote to Mrs. Sibley, & enclosed my Letter to Mr. [Michael] Eley, to whom I wrote in relation to the order on him in fav[o]r of the Kansas. I put the Letter in the charge of the head chief, who promises to deliver it safely to Mr. Eley. Having now finished all our business with the Kansas, we took leave of them and Set forward again upon our Survey. We are entirely out of Meat and must hasten on without unnecessary delay to the

Arkansas, where we hope to find buffalo. We traveled over a very level plain 12 Miles and 43 chains to the Little Arkansas, where we pitched our Tents on the bank of the River. Our Hunters killed several Buffalo today, but they were all very poor, and scarcely fit to eat. No other game killed today. The Little Arkansas is a clear, brisk running Stream, about 25 yards wide, Water Sweet and good. It is now very Shallow, the bed Sandy, banks high, a few Scattering Cotton Trees along on them. Pretty good pasturage.

Wednesday 17th August.—It rained a little last night, and is cloudy this morning. Musquetoes very troublesome here. Horses done rather poorly.

We set out at 8 o'Clk. after breakfast. Traveled 4¼ Miles over very rough flat ground, much cut up with ridges & holes & slashes, and reached the Sand Hills where we found plenty of good Water, and a great many Plums. After resting here two hours under some very large Spreading Cotton Trees (of which there are many in these Hills) we pursued our course & drove about 1¾ Miles through the Sands, and came to a rough Sandy Prairie, over which we traveled about 1 Mile further to another narrow range of Sand Hills, and then down into the great Arkansas Plain, upon which we rode about 2 Miles and came to a small river upon the bank of which we camped just at Sunset, and just as a heavy rain came on. We have traveled today 9 miles and 21 Chains. The Sand Hills are nothing like what they have been reported to be by travellers; in Extent they are not over two Miles where we crossed them, and of that not over half the distance is very difficult. It is certain however, that if we had pursued the Road that we left on Monday, we might have avoided these Hills entirely; and it is now Still more obvious that the best route of all would have been that mentioned in my Note of the 14th, turning off more Northward at Cotton Wood Grove. The Creek we are now on is called Cold Water Creek [Cow Creek]. It is nearly as large as the Little Arkansas, which it resembles very much. Its water is good and abundant; but there is no timber on it to be seen here. The Grass very good—*some* drift Wood.

Thursday 18th August.—A very heavy rain fell last Night. Still cloudy this morning. Started at six before Breakfast— traveled about 4 Miles, and arrived on the bank of the Arkansas—then kept up the River 2 Miles to a pile of drift wood and Halted to get Breakfast. The Arkansas is here about 500 yards wide from bank to bank, its bed sand, water turbid, current swift, channel full of Sand bars. One of the Men waded across, & found it in no place over four feet deep. Not a Tree to be seen on its banks.

At 3 P.M. we again Started, and continued up on the margin of the River about 4 Miles, and camped for the night on the bank, having measured 10 Miles and 2 Chains today.

The immense plain in which we now are, and through which the Arkansas flows, is almost an uninterrupted level as far as the eye can See to the South and West. The soil is apparently fertile and deep, the Herbage tolerably luxuriant; but there is not a single Tree anywhere to be seen on its banks. Our road this evening lay over some tolerably rough sandy ground, in which Rattle Snakes are very numerous. I observed this Morning as I passed through a Village (as it is called) of Prairie Dogs, several very luxuriant bunches of common Garden *Pursley*, & some A--e Smart. Saw a Hawk, Prairie Hen & Lark. *Heard* a Partridge. Gofers abundant. Killed a Buffalo in the River. The Grass indifferent here. Horses failing very fast.

Friday 19th August.—Morning fair and cool. After Breakfast we started at 8 o'Clk. Pursued our way up the River by its course pretty nearly, over very much the same kind of ground as yesterday, and after traveling 7 Miles and 51 Chains halted again on the River bank. The Horses very much jaded. Killed several fat Buffaloes today. Saw Deer, Goats, Hares, and Wolves. Buffalo getting very plenty. The River is here 54 yds. wide, no Tree seen yet. One of the Mules bit by a Rattle Snake this evening. These snakes are very numerous & troublesome here.

Saturday 20th August.—Morning fair & pleasant. We remained in camp all this day for the purpose of resting and recruiting the Horses, as the Grass is very good here. I have to Note that the circuitous distance from Ft. Osage to the Arkansas where we Struck it on Thursday the 18th is 262½ Miles as Measured. To this place it is 275 as traveled—213 Miles upon a straight line, on the course So[uth] 74 West. The Latitude here is 38°-11'-29". Longitude 98°. The River is on the fall. The Weather very fine.

Sunday 21st August.—Morning cool and fair—very heavy dew—the Night quite cool. Nearly opposite our camp, say 300 yds. above, a range of Sand Hills touches the River, some of which are covered with Plum bushes loaded with fruit, and about half a Mile below us on the North side are some other Hills of the same kind. Those on the South side of the River are the first that approach it on that side for about 20 Miles below. Above us in sight are a few Trees on the River. The pasturage in this plain is generally extremely fine. The Grass is soft, short and very nutricious, somewhat resembling the Blue Grass. The Ponds & slashes which are numerous a little

back from the River are slightly Saline, & the whole Plain is
believed to be so too—and it is from those causes that the
Grass is so remarkably nutricious, and so very much relished
by Horses, Buffalo, &c. At 8 o'Clk. we struck our Camp, &
again proceeded up the River in the Bottom Six Miles & 40
Chains & halted for the day. At 12 the Mercury stood at 84—at
6 P.M. it was 73.

Monday 22d August.—A very pleasant Morning. The Grass
being very good here, we Staid in Camp all day for the benefit
of the Horses; and it is necessary also to unload & examine
the Stores & Provisions, Issue some Blankets and Clothing to
the men, and Shoe some of the Horses. Our camp is opposite
a small Grove of Cotton Trees. The High ground [is] near the
River on the North Side. Some sand Hills still in sight. Mercury
84 at 12—64 at 6 P.M. Mr. Brown says the current of the
Arkansas is here about 2¼ Miles per hour.

Tuesday 23d August.—The morning fair and cool. Mercury
66 at 8 o'Clk. in the shade. At half an hour past Eight we
started again. The Waggons continued up the River in the
bottom. I rode out from the River upon the Hills to view the
country. First I went No[rth] E[ast] about a mile, which took
me quite out of the River bottom, and upon a high Ridge,
from which I had a fine view of the immense level Plain thro'
which the Arkansas runs.

I then went on nearly North, about 3 Miles over high
broken Prairie, and got on a high point of a Ridge, from which
I Saw off to the Eastward a string of Timber about 5 Miles off,
pointing out the course of a Creek, which I know to be the
one we left on the 18th called Cold Water [Cow Creek]. This
Creek appears to run nearly parallel with the Arkansas, and
takes its rise in a High dividing Ridge to the North; which
ridge I suppose to be the same that separates the Streams of
the Arkansas from those of the Kansas River, and upon which I
am of opinion the Road ought to run from the Cotton Wood
fork of the Nee Ozho to the Arkansas. I saw many Herds of
Buffalo scattered through the Rich meadow grounds over
towards the Creek; the Scenery is altogether very beautiful & I
enjoyed it the more as the morning was cool and pleasant. I
rode on a Mile or two farther towards the North, and then
turned more Westward, and fell into a beautiful & very
extensive Rich Valley or Meadow, having two small streams
running through it, and numerous herds of Buffalo grazing in
every direction. The soil in this Valley is very rich. The Grass
very thick & Luxuriant of the kind called Buffalo Grass, which
never grows tall. I presume the Valley may contain ten

thousand acres. It is all beautifully level & thickly set with Buffalo Grass, and looks like an immense field of Blue Grass.

The soil on the High land is much inferior to this in the Valley. On the declivity of one or two of the Ridges I noticed some Black Rocks; and in the course of my ride among the Hills I saw some very pretty flowers, a Small herd of Goats, a Hair, a Hawk, a Dog Town, several Buzzards, several Wolves, and two bea[u]tiful Water Birds resembling somewhat in shape & manner what we commonly call The Plover, but larger & nearly White. I also saw some Killdeers, and a small species of Hawk that is peculiar to the Dog Towns in which they reside. In one of those Towns I saw several large Rattlesnakes. I spent nearly an Hour in one of them, which is more than a league Square, I think, observing its curious Inhabitants. The Prairie Dog, as it is called from its barking like a Puppy, is about the size & colour of a Rabbit but resembles more the Gray Squirrel in other particulars. It burrows in the ground to a great depth, lives on grass, and in pairs. They are very wild and difficult to catch or to kill, tho' I made out to shoot one this morning. What is very curious is that the Dogs, Snakes, & Hawks all occupy the same dens—at least I have frequently seen them all run into the same Holes. How they agree together I cannot tell. It is certain that the Dogs are the right proprietors; & the Snakes & Hawks are no doubt intruders, for the purpose I presume of preying on the young Dogs.

I turned in towards the River & got there at 12, where I found the company encamped on the bank, Having drove today 9 Miles. At 12 the Mercury 84, at Sunset 74. The River rising fast.

Wednesday 24th August.—The Morning Cool and Hazy. Wind from the South. Mercury 70 at 7. River falling.

We left camp at 25 Min[utes] past 8. Kept up in the River bottom about 2 Miles, and passed a large Island thickly timbered with Cotton Wood, called the Pit Grove. We passed a few Scattering Trees below this; and above, the River is distinctly marked by those Trees as far as we can see. The Arkansas bottom not becomes much more confined on the No[rth] side, by the great dividing ridge Noticed yesterday; which is here about 3 Miles from the River. We continued onward, and at 12, got to The Walnut Creek, called 6 miles above the Pit Grove.

We crossed the Creek at a good ford, not far from the mouth, and camped on the bank in a Bend, among some Scattering Walnuts and Elms, where we found very excellent pasturage and plenty of fuel. The Creek is about 20 Yards wide. Water clear & good, and plenty. Distance traveled today 8 Miles & 25 Chains—the Road very good all the way.

Thursday 25th August.—The norming fair & pleasant. Busy all day writing and gathering seeds. Buffalo passing all day near camp—several fat ones killed. At a short distance from camp, the men get great quantities of very fine Plums. Horses doing very well here. We intend to stay several days. The day generally cloudy & warm. John Walker lost his Horse, saddle & blankets. He ran off with a gang of Buffalo.

Friday 26th August.—Morning Hazy & Cloudy. Cleared off at 9, & proved a fine day tho' very Warm. Busy Writing all day. Many of the Men out killing Buffalo.

The Latitude of this place ascertained to be 38°-21'-10". The distance as measured from Ft. Osage is 299 Miles. It is South 57 Miles & West 244 Miles from Ft. O[sage]. The direct course from Ft. O[sage] to W[alnut] Creek is South 77° West and the distance on that course air measure is 250 Miles. At 12 o'Clk. today the Mercury stood at 86—at 10 P.M. it was 76.

Saturday 27th August.—Very fine morning. After early Breakfast Mr. Brown, Mr. Gamble & myself set out on an excursion Northward, over the Ridge, to ascertain the relative position of the Kansas & Arkansas Rivers which are laid down on the Maps as coming close together at this point. Mr. B[rown] took his Instruments with him to get the Latitude. Capt. Cooper and Williams accompanied us. We rode North about 3 Miles, and ascended the Ridge—then over the ridge ab[ou]t 1½ Mile same course, and descended into an extensive low flat Prairie [Cheyenne Bottoms] through which [we] continued about 4 Miles, passing through a marsh half a mile across, & came to a Small Creek running South East, towards a Large Lake which is seen about 2 Miles off in that direction. We continued on the same course, after crossing the Creek, for about a Mile, and came to a large Pond [northern body of marsh], then we turned more westward, and in a short distance came to the Same Creek [Deception Creek] again at a Bend. Coursed the Creek upward in a direction about No[rth] W[est] by W]est half a Mile, then turned off nearly West ¼ Mile, and came to a Creek [Blood Creek] having some Ash timber on it. These two Creeks lose themselves in the Marsh through which we passed. The Marsh drains itself into the Large Lake, and it is probable (as William asserts) that the Smoky Hill Fork receives a principal supply of Water from this Lake. The Creek we are now on is but small, not over 15 yds. Wide. Its banks are high, and though there is but little Water in it at present, it runs briskly; and from the great piles of Heavy drift Wood seen along its Banks, I should judge it to be a pretty long & at times a considerable Stream. It is very much inferior however to the River laid down on the Maps as the Smoke Hill Fork. I am inclined to believe that there is still another and a Larger stream a few Miles farther North, beyond a High Ridge just by—but the day is so excessively Hot that I Shall decline any further Search at this time. It is certain that the Creek [Blood Creek] we are now on is a branch of the Kansas River,* & the nearest of any other to the Arkansas. Mr. Brown got the Latitude with tolerable precision, which is 38°-30'-29"—so that the distance across from this Creek to the Arkansas is 10¾ Miles.

The Mercury was up to 88 at 12. We staid in the shade about 2 Hours, and then set out on our return to camp. We rode up the Creek about 2 Miles—then crossed it and traveled about South West, nearly 2 Miles, thro' a level dry Bottom— then ascended a High Ridge [North of Great Bend], then pursued our course down a very gently inclined Plane, about 4 Miles to the Walnut Creek, which we find rising very fast. We kept down the Creek about 8 Miles, and arrived at Camp just at sunset having traveled today nearly 30 Miles. The Creek was nearly swimming & rising very fast. Current swift, Water muddy, Drift wood passing. As far as I have been able to examine this Creek today, it has a thin growth of Ash, Walnut, Elm, & Box Elder & Cotton Wood Timber all along its banks. A Mr. [Nathaniel Miguel] Pryor arrived at our camp today, with three other Men, on their way to New New [sic] Mexico on a Trapping expedition. They came up the Arkansas from Cantonment Gibson.

Sunday 28th August.—There fell a very heavy rain last night accompanied with high wind. We got everything wet in the Tents. The morning fair but very Warm—Mercury 74 at 9. After getting our baggage dried, which was not effected till 12 o'Clock, we struck our Camp at 1 P.M. and moved onward. Traveled over a rough and uneven bottom, near the River 6 Miles & 78 Chains, and halted on the bank [in vicinity of Great Bend] for the Night. The Timber of Walnut Creek, a southern fork, appears in sight all the way at about 3 miles distance from the River. The day very Hot. The Mercury 88 at 12.

Monday 29th August.—The morning very clear and Warm. The River pretty full & rising. At 7 the Mercury stood at 72.

---

*"Not so certain as since ascent. It may be the 'Cold Water' Creek." [Sibley's note.]

After breakfast, we started at 45 Min[utes] past 8. Traveled over very rough & uneven ground, through the bottom, very much cut up with wet slashes. The Grass is rough and coarse and very much overrun with Weeds. The Walnut Creek still appears in sight, and is about 5 Miles from the Arkansas. At half past 12 we halted on a small Creek [Ash Creek], near its mouth, having measured today 10 Miles and 46 Chains. The water clear & good in the Creek, but no timber to be seen on it. At 1 P.M. the Mercury was at 88. Buffalo very numerous.

Tuesday 20th August.—The morning clear cool and pleasant, a fine air stir[r]ing. The Creek very high, & still rising, the water very muddy & filthy.

After Breakfast at 30 Min[utes] past 8, we all started. The Waggons and most of the Party kept up the River Bottom. Mr. Gamble and myself rode out upon the high Prairie. We first rode nearly north about a mile to a remarkable Rocky Point [Pawnee Rock] which projects into the Bottom from a High Ridge; these Rocks are very large and of a glossy Black colour; Towards the River, the face is nearly perpendicular. We rode upon the top which is probably 50 feet above the plain below, and from whence there is a charming view of the country in every direction. After we had sufficiently gratified our curiosity here, we proceeded Northward across several Ridges, about two miles farther, and came in full view of an immense level flat. We halted to note the beautiful prospect that here presented itself. The Walnut Creek we Saw distinctly mapped below us. We could see that it forks, and that both principal forks run from the West, the southern one rather from So[uth] W[est] so that the whole appearance of the Creek here is somewhat like a Semicircle. Mr. G[amble] and I went down through the Valley steering a little more West to the Creek which we crossed, and stopped a couple of hours in the Shade of Some Trees, having rode about 10 Miles about No[rth] 45 W[est] from the Camp we started from. We then rode 2 Miles up between the forks; then crossed the Southern one, and steered So[uth] W[est] about 3 Miles then more South 2 Miles and came in sight of a long string of Timber stretching from So[uth] W[est] to No[rth] E[ast], which proves to be the Creek that we left this morning. This we reached about 10 Miles above where we camped last Night, and coursed it down 'till we found the company camped on the North Bank, it being too full to cross the Waggons today. The distance measured today is only 7 M[iles] & 60 Ch[ain]s. The Rocky point is still in plain view about 5 miles to the Eastward. This Creek is extremely Crooked, and well deserves the name we have given it "Crooked Creek" [Ash Creek]. As far as I could see up it, there is Timber—and this is also the case with all the branches of Walnut Creek.

We saw a great many Buffalo today, several Horses, and a variety of other Smaller Game.

Wednesday 31st August.—The morning cool and cloudy and Windy. The principal timber of this & the Walnut Creek, where I saw them yesterday, is Ash, Elm, Box Elder & Cotton. The Creek having run down so that the Waggons can cross, we Set off again after Breakfast at half past 8. Our way was over rather broken Prairie, and at a greater distance from the River than we usually Travel. At half past 10 we reached the Pawnee fork, and camped on the bank, a little below the fording place, at Some large Elm Trees, having measured from the last camp 6 M[ile]s & 56 Ch[ain]s. A heavy rain fell while we were on the road. The Creek appears to be too full now to venture to cross it with the Waggons; besides the banks require some digging at the ford. Here we have a beautiful camping place, & very fine range for the Horses.

Thursday 1t September.—The morning cloudy and cool. Mercury 68 at 8 o'Clock. The Pawnee River is here about 40 yards wide, banks pretty high, bottom sandy, Water at present Muddy. Timber Elm, Ash, Elder, Cotton Tree, Willow, and Grape Vines. Yesterday I turned off from the direct course and struck the Arkansas at the mouth of this River, and then coursed it up about a Mile to the fording place near which we are now encamped, which is just at the foot of a high rocky Hill. The path leading up from the mouth to the ford passes betweeen the Pawnee and some Cliffs of Soft Rock, upon the smooth faces of which are cut the names of many Persons, who have at different times passed this way to and from New Mexico. Some Indian marks are also to be seen on these Rocks. This ford of Pawnee River is 31 Miles from Walnut Creek, & 330 from Ft. Osage. The direct course from Ft. Osage is South 74 West.

Apprehending more Rain and fearing to be detained here by high water, we set to work cutting down the Banks, and preparing the ford for the Waggons to cross. We got all safe over without any accident or much difficulty by 11 o'Clk. and then proceeded South West through a flat bottom about 6 Miles, and came to a High Ridge. The Waggons passed round the point, still keeping in the bottom about half a mile from the River. I rode upon the Ridge, from the top of which, I could distinctly trace the course of the Pawnee River for a great distance by the fringe of Trees along its banks. Its general course as far as I could see is from So[uth] W[est] to No[rth] E[ast]. It runs nearly parallel with the Arkansas at an average distance of about Six Miles apart, gradually diverging.

The traveling today is pretty good. There is no interruption along the River Bottom, except one little muddy Creek that intervenes about 3 Miles above the crossing of Pawnee Creek [Saw Mill Creek]. The Grass is very good, but Buffalo are scarce, which seems to indicate the recent presence of Indians, tho' we have not discovered any *other* Signs of any. I presume that some of the Pawnees and Recaras may have been in this quarter not long since, this being the usual Summer Resort of those People particularly the Pawnees. But it is more than probable I think, that they have now all retuned to their Villages to gather their Corn &c.

We encamped on a Small Creek near its mouth affording plenty of good Water & fine grass. We call it Clear Creek [Big Coon Creek, near Garfield] from the quality of its water. The distance traveled today as measured is 11 Miles.

Friday 2d. September.—It rained nearly all night and continued to rain nearly all this day. We staid in camp, and spent an uncomfortable day—the Mercury about 65 all day. At night the Horses all took fright & ran furiously into camp. The cause could not be ascertained, tho' it was probably a Wolf or a Buffalo.

Saturday 3d September.—A very fine clear cool Morning. The Mercury 62 at 7. After drying our Baggage, we struck our Tents and moved on at 10 Min[utes] past 9. The Waggons still kept along in the bottom. I rode off more Westward upon the high Ridges, from some of which, I again had a good view of the Pawnee fork, which still appears to run from So[uth] W[est] to No[rth] E[ast]. It is here about 10 Miles from the Arkansas. Before I left the River Bottom, I passed over an extensive tract near the foot of the Ridge, a little elevated above the flat bottom, containing perhaps a thousand Acres or more; all over which, I observed piles of coarse gravel and hard stones, some of the latter as large as Hen's Eggs. These were thrown out by the Prairie Dogs and Ants. The surface of this Tract is generally a tolerably Rich sandy loam producing very good grass. I have frequently seen the same appearances in the Bottom before; and the banks of the Arkansas often present the very Same kinds of Gravel & Stones, some 18 or 20 Inches below the Surface. The Highland seen today is *waving* as 'tis called—being a Succession of Ridges, running irregularly, some of which present themselves with abrupt steep points upon the River bottom.

The Arkansas still keeps its width of from 400 to 500 yards, and in other respects is very much as where we first saw it—with the exception of its being better furnished with Timber. Its course can now be traced distinctly for a great distance, by the few scattering Cotton Trees (there are no other) that are Scattered along its Banks & upon its little Islands; and this is the case all the way from about 20 Miles below the Walnut Creek. Since we crossed the Pawnee fork, the appearance of the country on the south side of the Arkansas is much more rough and hilly, and in general the Hills are closer to the River on both sides. I saw six Wild Horses today on the high Prairie & shot at them, but without effect. Buffalo are scarce; tho' our Hunters manage to kill a sufficiency of fine fat Cows for the company. At 2 P.M. the Mercury was at 80. I then turned in to the River, and found the Party encamped on the Bank. In passing from the Hills to the River through the bottom, I crossed the Clear Creek twice. It is a very pretty, brisk running Creek. Williams who has been hunting today over the River came in just as Sunset with a fat Elk. The distance measured today is 11 Miles & 68 Chains.

Sunday 4th September.—Morning clear & cool and windy—the Wind from the South. Mercury 66 at 7.

Started the Waggons at 10 M[inutes] past 9. Traveled up the River pretty nearly by its course, in the bottom. High Hills and Nobs on the opposite side, some of which are of loose naked Sand. The Hills on the North side are about 3 Miles from the River. The Clear Creek runs down through the bottom about midway between the Hills and the River. I saw and Crossed it frequently during my Zig Zag ride today; it still appears brisk & *flush* and its water clear & good. Its bed gravelly in many places. The Waggons kept along between the Creek and the River—road good. The Bottom is very much the same where we traveled today as usual, as respects soil and Grass &c. The River is also nearly the same in its width, depth and general appearance. Several very fat cows killed today, and an Elk and a Deer also killed, these latter are but rarely seen in these rejions [sic]. Our Men kill daily as much fine beef as would Subsist an army. And yet Buffalo are, comparatively, very scarce where we are now traveling. Halted and encamped on the River bank—distance today 12 M[ile]s 28 Ch[ain]s.

Monday 5th September.—Morning clear, calm & sultry. Mercury 76 at 8. Started at 9. I rode out to the Hills about 3 Miles, and then kept along upon the high Prairie, nearly parallel with the River about 10 Miles, and returned to the River in the evening. The country not much broken, but very pretty. I saw several Horses and Goats & many Buffalo.

From the High Ridges I could see the Sand Hills on the other side of the River. Some of them are quite large, & some quite naked. These when the sun shone bright on them looked like so many Pillars of fire. Distance measured today 12 Miles and 27 Chains.

Tuesday 6th September.—A severe Storm of Wind and Rain last night—the morning clear & very windy—the Mercury 65 at 7 o'Clk. We started at 9. I again left the company and rode out upon the High Prairie, but saw nothing today worthy of notice, except some chalky looking Rocks. After riding about 5 Miles over the broken Hills, excessively annoyed by the wind, I turned down into the River bottom, and went to the River at a Remarkable Rocky Point or Cliff on the North Side [opposite Ford], close to which the River runs. About 2 Miles above this, I fell in with the Waggons, encamped on the River bank nearly opposite the Mouth of a Creek which enters the Arkansas on the south side, known by the name of Mulberry Creek. The distance measured today is only 4 Miles and 55 Chains.

Wednesday 7th September.—The morning calm and pleasant. Mercury from 50 to 89 between 6 & 12. Staid in camp all day. We are in a small bottom almost encircled by Hills on the North Side—the Pasturage very good & fuel plenty. Our Camp is in the extreme South bend of the River— Latitude 37°-38'-52", Longitude about 99° agreeably to Mr. Brown's calculations and measurement. Distance south 107⅛ Miles. West 300½ from Ft. Osage. The distance as measured & traveled is 383 Miles. General course South 70¼ West, and the distance upon that course 314 Miles from Ft. Osage. Distance lost by circuitous travel 79 Miles.

Thursday 8th September.—Very warm morning—fair and calm. Being so near the boundary line now, where we must wait for further Instructions from our Gov[ernmen]t, we are in no haste to move on very fast, especially as the Weather is very Warm, our Horses tired and poor and Several of them actually given out. As the Grass is Still good here, we will remain at this camp 'till tomorrow. Game is Scare around here, but we manage to kill sufficient. The River is about 350 yards wide here, very Shallow, & full of very small Islands. The country opposite pretty level.

Mulberry Creek runs from the South West. It is said to be very short, not over 20 Miles, & its head branches interlock with those of the Grand Saline [Branch of Cimarron] which runs parallel with the Arkansas about 30 Miles from it at this point. At least such is the report of two of our Men who have been across there.

Friday 9th September.—The morning cool and pleasant. Raised our camp & started onward at 10 o'Clk. Proceeded up the river 12 Miles and 33 Chains, and halted on the bank at a point where the Hills close in upon the River, just at the mouth of a Ravine or small drain. The River is wider here than just below, & has many small Islands. The Prairie opposite & for several miles below is low and flat. We were obliged to leave one of the Horses this Morning, Lame, tired, poor and Sick.

Saturday 10th September.—The morning cool and fair and very windy. Started at 10 minutes past 10. We proceeded up the Bottom, which still continues to get narrower on the North side—the River full of small islands on some of the largest of which are a few Cotton Trees.

We had rode about 10 Miles, when we came to a large Mass of Gravel Rock of a very remarkable appearance. It presents itself at the termination of a High Ridge and faces the River from which it is about a Mile; a level flat intervening. Its front is rough & broken, & about 200 yards in extent. To judge from appearances, one might suppose that the Arkansas once washed the base of this Rock; but this would involve the supposition that the present bed of the River has been sunk by some convulsion of nature not less than Fifty feet—to justify which, I could discover nothing. The Rock as it is seen at the Bluff is in large Masses, which are composed of small Gravel Stones and Sand firmly cemented together. These stones when separated generally appear firmly polished, like those found in the beds of Rivers. They are in great varieties as to Colour, Size and Substance. In the mixture there is evidently Lime.

We passed this curious Rock, and then Shaped our course South West over Wet Prairie to the River, and Pitched our Tents on the Bank, just below a high Bluff Bank [3 miles beyond Caches], which is near Some Cotton Trees. The wind very boisterous all day. Distance measured 13 Miles & 13 Chains.

Josiah Gregg's book actually covers a number of trips and years. The excerpts included here cover one trip made in 1831. He describes difficulties in stream crossings, accidents and medical treatment, order of march, settings up camp, prairie animals, and cacheing goods. His party left Independence on May 15, 1831, and was at the Arkansas by July 1st. They reached The Caches on July 18th.

Early the next day we reached the 'Little Arkansas,' which, although endowed with an imposing name, is only a small creek with a current but five or six yards wide. But, though small, its steep banks and miry bed annoyed us exceedingly in crossing. It is the practice upon the prairies on all such occasions, for several men to go in advance with axes, spades and mattocks, and, by digging the banks and erecting temporary bridges, to have all in readiness by the time the wagons arrive. A bridge over a quagmire is made in a few minutes, by cross-laying it with brush (willows are best, but even long grass is often employed as a substitute), and covering it with earth,—across which a hundred wagons will often pass in safety.

We had now arrived at the point nearest to the border, I believe, where any outrages have been perpetrated upon the traders to Santa Fe. One of the early packing companies lost their animals on this spot, and had to send back for a new supply.

Next day we reached Cow creek, where all the difficulties encountered at Little Arkansas had to be reconquered: but after digging, bridging, shouldering the wheels, with the usual accompaniment of whooping, swearing and cracking of whips, we soon got safely across and encamped in the valley beyond. Alarms now began to accumulate more rapidly upon us. A couple of persons had a few days before been chased to the wagons by a band of—buffalo; and this evening the encampment was barely formed when two hunters came bolting in with information that a hundred, perhaps of the same 'enemy,' were at hand—at least this was the current opinion afterwards. The hubbub occasioned by this fearful news had scarely subsided, when another arrived on a panting horse, crying out "Indians! Indians! I've just escaped from a couple, who pursued me to the very camp!" "To arms! to arms!" resounded from every quarter—and just then a wolf, attracted by the fumes of broiling buffalo bones, sent up a most hideous howl across the creek. "Some one in distress!" was instantly shouted: "To his relief!" vociferated the crown— and off they bolted, one and all, arms in hand, hurly-burley— leaving the camp entirely unprotected; so that had an enemy been at hand indeed, and approached us from the opposite direction, they might easily have taken possession of the wagons. Before they had all returned, however, a couple of hunters came in and laughed very heartily at the expense of the first alarmist, whom they had just chased into the camp.

Half a day's drive after leaving this camp of 'false alarms' brought us to the valley of Arkansas river. This point is about 270 miles from Independence. From the adjacent heights the landscape presents an imposing and picturesque appearance.

Beneath a ledge of wave-like yellow sandy ridges and hillocks spreading far beyond, descends the majestic river (averaging at least a quarter of a mile in width), bespeckled with verdant islets, thickly set with cottonwood timber. The banks are very low and barren, with the exception of an occasional grove of stunted trees, hiding behind a swamp or sand-hill, placed there as it were to protect it from the fire of the prairies, which in most parts keeps down every perennial growth. In many places, indeed, where there are no islands, the river is so entirely bare of trees, that the unthinking traveller might appraoch almost to its very brink, without suspecting its presence.

Thus far, many of the prairies have a fine and productive appearance, though the Neosho river (or Council Grove) seems to form the western boundary of the truly rich and beautiful country of the border. Up to that point the prairies are similar to those of Missouri—the soil equally exuberant and fertile; while all the country that lies beyond, is of a far more barren character—vegetation of every kind is more stinted—the gay flowers more scarce, and the scanty timber of a very inferior quality: indeed, the streams, from Council Grove westward, are lined with very little else than cotton-wood, barely interspersed here and there with an occasional elm or hackberry.

Following up the course of this stream for some twenty miles, now along the valley, and again traversing the points of protecting eminences, we reached Walnut creek. I have heard of a surgical operation performed at this point, in the summer of 1826, which, though not done exactly *secundum artem*, might suggest some novel reflections to the man of science. A few days before the caravan had reached this place, a Mr. Broadus, in attempting to draw his rifle from a wagon muzzle foremost, discharged its contents into his arm. The bone being dreadfully shattered, the unfortunate man was advised to submit to an amputation at once; otherwise, it being in the month of August, and excessively warm, mortification would soon ensue. But Broadus obstinately refused to consent to this course, till death began to stare him in the face. By this time, however, the whole arm had become gangrened, some spots having already appeared above the place where the operation should have been performed. The invalid's case was therefore considered perfectly hopeless, and he was given up by all his comrades, who thought of little else than to consign him to the grave.

But being unwilling to resign himself to the fate which appeared frowning over him, without a last effort, he obtained the consent of two or three of the party, who undertook to amputate his arm merely to gratify the wishes of the dying man; for in such a light they viewed him. There only 'case of instruments' consisted of a handsaw, a butcher's knife and a large iron bolt. The teeth of the saw being considered too coarse, they went to work, and soon had a set of fine teeth filed on the back. The knife having been whetted keen, and the iron bolt laid upon the fire, they commenced the operation: and in less time than it takes to tell it, the arm was opened round to the bone, which was almost in an instant sawed off; and with the whizzing hot iron the whole stump was so effectually seared as to close the arteries completely. Bandages were now applied, and the company proceeded on their journey as though nothing had occurred. The arm commenced healing rapidly, and in a few weeks the patient was sound and well, and is perhaps still living, to bear witness to the superiority of the 'hot iron' over ligatures, in 'taking up' arteries.

On the following day our route lay mostly over a level plain, which usually teems with buffalo, and is beautifully adapted to the chase. At the distance of about fifteen miles, the attention of the traveller is directed to the 'Pawnee Rock,' so called, it is said, on account of a battle's having once been fought hard by, between the Pawnees and some other tribe. It is situated at the projecting point of a ridge, and upon its surface are furrowed, in uncouth but legible characters, numerous dates, and the names of various travellers who have chanced to pass that way.

We encamped at Ash creek, where we again experienced sundry alarms in consequence of 'Indian sign,' that was discovered in the creek valley, such as unextinguished fires, about which were found some old moccasins,—a sure indication of the recent retreat of savages from the vicinity. These constant alarms, however, although too frequently the result of groundless and unmanly fears, are not without their salutary effects upon the party. They serve to keep one constantly on the alert, and to sharpen those faculties of observation which would otherwise become blunted or inactive. Thus far also we had marched in two lines only; but, after crossing the Pawnee Fork, each of the four divisions drove on in a separate file, which became henceforth the order of march till we reached the border of the mountains. By moving in long lines as we did before, the march is continually interrupted; for every accident which delays a wagon ahead stops all those behind. By marching four abreast, this difficulty is partially obviated, and the wagons can also be thrown more readily into a condition of defence in case of attack.

Upon encamping the wagons are formed into a 'hollow square' (each division to a side), constituting at once an enclosure (or *corral*) for the animals when needed, and a fortification against the Indians. Not to embarrass this cattle-pen, the camp fires are all lighted outside of the wagons. Outside of the wagons, also, the travellers spread their beds, which consist, for the most part, of buffalo-rugs and blankets. Many content themselves with a single Mackinaw; but a pair constitutes the most regular pallet; and he that is provided with a buffalo-rug into the bargain, is deemed luxuriously supplied. It is most usual to sleep out in the open air, as well to be at hand in case of attack, as indeed for comfort; for the serene sky of the Prairies affords the most agreeable and wholesome canopy. That deleterious attribute of night air and dews, so dangerous in other climates, is but little experienced upon the high plains: on the contrary, the serene evening air seems to affect the health rather favorably than otherwise. Tents are so rare on these expeditions that, in a caravan of two hundred men, I have not seen a dozen. In time of rain the traveller resorts to his wagon, which affords a far more secure shelter than a tent; for if the latter is not beaten down by the storms which so often accompany rain upon the prairies, the ground underneath is at least apt to be flooded. During dry weather, however, even the invalid prefers the open air.

Prior to the date of our trip, it had been customary to secure the horses by hoppling them. The 'fore-hopple' (a leathern strap or rope manacle upon the fore legs) being most convenient, was more frequently used; though the 'side-line' (a hopple connecting a fore and a hindleg) is the most secure; for with this an animal can hardly increase his pace beyond a hobbling walk; whereas, with the fore-hopple, a frighted horse will scamper off with nearly as much velocity as though he were unshackled. But, better than either of these is the practice which the caravans have since adopted of tethering the mules at night around the wagons, at proper intervals, with ropes twenty-five or thirty feet in length, tied to stakes fifteen to twenty inches long, driven into the ground; a supply of which, as well as mallets, the wagoners always carry with them.

It is amusing to witness the disputes which often arise among wagoners about their 'staking ground.' Each teamster is allowed, by our 'common law,' a space of about a hundred yards immediately fronting his wagon, which he is ever ready to defend, if a neighbor shows a disposition to encroach upon his soil. If any animals are found 'staked' beyond the 'chartered limits,' it is the duty of the guard to 'knock them up,' and turn them into the *corral*. Of later years the tethering of oxen has also been resorted to with advantage. It was thought at first that animals thus confined by ropes could not procure a sufficient supply of food; but experience has allayed all apprehension on the subject. In fact, as the camp is always pitched in the most luxuriantly clothed patches of prairie that can be selected, a mule is seldom able to despatch in the course of one night, all the grass within his reach. Again, when animals are permitted to range at liberty, they are apt to mince and nibble at the tenderest blades and spend their time in roaming from point to point, in search of what is most agreeable to their 'epicurean palates;' whereas if they are restricted by a rope, they will at once fall to with earnestness and clip the pasturage as it comes.

Although the buffalo had been scarce for a few days,—frightened off, no doubt, by the Indians whose 'sign' we saw about Ash creek, they soon became exceedingly abundant. The larger droves of these animals are sometimes a source of great annoyance to the caravans as, by running near our loose stock, there is frequent danger of their causing *stampedes* (or general scamper), in which case mules, horses and oxen have been known to run away among the buffalo, as though they had been a gang of their own species. A company of traders, in 1824, lost twenty or thirty of their animals in this way. Hunters have also been deprived of their horses in the same way. Leaping from them in haste, in order to take a more determinate aim at a buffalo, the horse has been known to take fright, and, following the fleeing game, has disappeared with saddle, bridle, pistols and all—most probably never to be heard of again. In fact, to look for stock upon these prairies, would be emphatically to 'search for a needle in a haystack;' not only because they are virtually boundless, but that being everywhere alive with herds of buffalo, from which horses cannot be distinguished at a distance, one knows not whither to turn in search after the stray animals.

We had lately been visited by frequent showers of rain, and upon observing the Arkansas river, it was found to be rising, which seemed portentous of the troubles which the 'June freshet' might occasion us in crossing it; and, as it was already the 11th of this month, this annual occurrence was now hourly expected. On some occasions caravans have been obliged to construct what is called a buffalo boat, which is done by stretching the hides of these animals over a frame of

poles, or, what is still more common, over an empty wagon-
body. The 'June freshets,' however, are seldom of long
duration; and, during the greatest portion of the year, the
channel is very shallow. Still the bed of the river being in
many places filled with quicksand, it is requisite to examine
and mark out the best ford with stakes, before one undertakes
to cross. The wagons are then driven over usually by double
teams, which should never be permitted to stop, else animals
and wagons are apt to founder, and the loading is liable to be
damaged. I have witnessed a whole team down at once,
rendering it necessary to unharness and drag each mule out
separately: in fact, more than common exertion is sometimes
required to prevent these dumpish animals from drowning in
their fright and struggles through the water, though the
current be but shallow at the place. Hence it is that oxen are
much safer for fording streams than mules. As for ourselves,
we forded the river without serious difficulty.

Rattlesnakes are proverbially abundant upon all these
prairies, and as there is seldom to be found either stick or
stone with which to kill them, one hears almost a constant
popping of rifles or pistols among the vanguard, to clear the
route of these disagreeable occupants, lest they should bite
our animals. As we were toiling up through the sandy hillocks
which border the southern banks of the Arkansas, the day
being exceedingly warm, we came upon a perfect den of these
reptiles. I will not say 'thousands,' though this perhaps were
nearer the truth—but hundreds at least were coiled or
crawling in every direction. They were no sooner discovered
than we were upon them with guns and pistols, determined to
let none of them escape.

In the midst of this amusing scramble among the snakes, a
wild mustang colt, which had, somehow or other, become
separated from its dam, came bolting among our relay of
loose stock to add to the confusion. One of our mules,
evidently impressed with the impertinence of the intruder,
sprang forward and attacked it, with the apparent intention of
executing summary chastisement; while another mule, with
more benignity of temper than its irascible compeer, engaged
most lustily in defence of the unfortunate little mustang. As
the contest was carried on among the wagons, the teamsters
soon became very uproarious; so that the whole, with the
snake fracas, made up a capital scene of confusion. When the
mule skirmish would have ended, if no one had interfered, is
a question which remained undetermined; for some of our
company, in view of the consequences that might result from
the contest, rather inhumanly took sides with the assailing

mule; and soon after they entered the lists, a rifle ball relieved the poor colt from its earthly embarrassments, and the company from further domestic disturbance. Peace once more restored, we soon got under way, and that evening pitched our camp opposite the celebrated 'Caches,' a place where some of the earliest adventures had been compelled to conceal their merchandise.

The history of the origin of these 'Caches' may be of sufficient interest to merit a brief recital. Beard, of the unfortunate party of 1812, alluded to in the first chapter, having returned to the United States in 1822, together with Chambers, who had descended the Canadian river the year before, induced some small capitalists of St. Louis to join in an enterprise, and then undertook to return to Santa Fe the same fall, with a small party and an assortment of merchandise. Reaching the Arkansas late in the season, they were overtaken by a heavy snow storm, and driven to take shelter on a large island. A rigorous winter ensued, which forced them to remain pent up in that place for three long months. During this time the greater portion of their animals perished; so that, when the spring began to open, they were unable to continue their journey with their goods. In this emergency they made a *cache* some distance above, on the north side of the river, where they stowed away the most of their merchandise. From thence they proceeded to Taos, where they procured mules, and returned to get their hidden property.

Few travellers pass this way without visiting these mossy pits, many of which remain partly unfilled to the present day. In the vicinity, or a few miles to the eastward perhaps, passes the hundredth degree of longitude west from Greenwich, which, from the Arkansas to Red River, forms the boundary between the United States and the Mexican, or rather the Texan territory.

The term *cache*, meaning a *place of concealment*, was originally used by the Canadian French trappers and traders. It is made by digging a hole in the ground, somewhat in the shape of a jug, which is lined with dry sticks, grass, or anything else that will protect its contents from the dampness of the earth. In this place the goods to be concealed are carefully stowed away; and the aperture is then so effectually closed as to protect them from the rains. In *caching*, a great deal of skill is often required, to leave no signs whereby the cunning savage might discover the place of deposit. To this end, the excavated earth is carried to some distance and carefully concealed, or thrown into a stream if one be at hand.

The place selected for a cache is usually some rolling piont, sufficiently elevated to be secure from inundations. If it be well set with grass, a solid piece of turf is cut out large enough for the entrance. The turf is afterward laid back, and taking root, in a short time no signs remain of its ever having been molested. However, as every locality does not afford a turfy site, the camp fire is sometimes built upon the place, or the animals are penned over it, which effectually destroys all traces of the cache.

Susan Magoffin headed west in 1846 from the Independence area on June 10, 1846 with her new husband, trader Samuel Magoffin. This was her honeymoon. She referred to her husband, Samuel, by the affectionate term "Mi alma" (My soul). She traveled more luxuriously then most others. Her concerns reflected her sex, age, new family status, and the wartime tensions of the Mexican war. Prairie animals, death on the trail, stream crossing problems, and illness are all mentioned. By July 1, 1846, she was near the Arkansas, and by July 18, she arrived at The Caches.

Noon. 21. Little Cow Creek. July 1, 1846. According to the calculation of Mr. Gregg, a gentleman who made several expeditions across the Prairies and who wrote a history of the trade &c, we are 249 miles from Independence.

We camped last night at Arrow Rock creek—most of our travel yesterday was after 5 o'clock P.M. till 10–8 miles. I was quite sick and took medicine which has made me feel like a new being today. I am at least *50 per cent better.*

We had a fine dinner today and I enjoyed it exceedingly, for I had eaten nothing but a little tea and half a biscuit since yesterday dinner. It consisted of boiled chicken, soup, rice, and a dessert of *wine and gooseberry tart.* Such a thing on the plains would be looked upon by those at home as an utter impossibility. But nevertheless it is true. Jane and I went off as soon as we got here and found enough to make a fine pie. I wish the plumbs and grapes were ripe; there is any quantity of them along all the little streams we pass.

One of the wagoners chased a wolf today. We see them frequently lurking about, ready to come pick the scraps, if the dogs chance to leave any, where we have camped.

Camped tonight at big Cow Creek, three miles from the

other which we left at seven o'clock. The crossing here is very bad and took us till moon down to cross. It is good water and wood, so we struck camp.

Camp No. 22. Bank of the Arkansas River. Prairie scenes are rather changing today. We are coming more into the buffalo regions. The grass is much shorter and finer. The plains are cut up by winding paths and every thing promises a *buffalo dinner* on the *4th*.

We left our last night's camp quite early this morning. About 9 o'clock we came upon "Dog City," This curiosity is well worth seeing. The Prairie dog, not much larger than a well grown rat, burrows in the ground. They generally make a regular town of it, each one making his house by digging a hole, and heaping the dirt around the mouth of this. Two are generally built together in a neighbourly way. They of course visit as regularly as man. When we got into this one, which lays on both sides of the road occupying at least a circle of some hundred yards, the little fellows like people ran to their doors to see the passing crowd. They could be seen all around with their heads poked out, and expressing their opinions I supposed from the loud barking I heard.

We nooned it on the Prairie without water for the cattle, within sight of the river, but some six miles from it. The banks are quite sandy and white, having the appearance, at a distance, of a large city. It is shaded by the trees in some places, having very much the appearance of white and coloured houses.

Came to camp tonight before sunset. Col. Owens' Company, which got before us this morning, were just starting after performing the last office to the dead body of a Mexican. He had consumption. Poor man, 'twas but yesterday that we sent him some soup from our camp, which he took with relish and today he is in his grave!

The manner of interring on the plains is necessarily very simple. The grave is dug very deep, to prevent the body from being found by the wolves. The corpse is rolled in a blanket—lowered and stones put on it. The earth is then thrown in, the sod replaced and it is well beat down. Often the corral is made over it, to make the earth still more firm, by the tromping of the stock. The Mexicans always place a cross at the grave.

Our camp is on the bank of the Arkansas tonight. Its dark waters remind me of the Mississippi.—It makes me sad to look upon it.—I am reminded of home. Though the Mississippi is a vast distance from there—it seems to me a

near neighbour, compared with the distance I am from it—
now three hundred miles from Independence. The time rolls
on so fast I can scarcely realize its three weeks out.

Camp No. 23. This has indeed been a long day's travel. We
left the Arkansas river, along which we have been traveling far
and near since we first struck it, this morning by a little after 6
o'clock, and by 10 o'clock reached the Walnut Creek, a branch
of the Arkansas, and eight miles from it. Crossed it with ease,
the water quite deep though—and nooned it 4 miles farther
near the Arkansas. Today I have seen the first time wild
buffalo. A herd of some ten or 12 were just across the river
from our nooning place. The teamsters all afire to have a
chase started off half a dozen of them—and much to our
surprise, for we expected nothing of the kind, killed one—so
after all we are to have a buffalo dinner tomorrow.

Started this P.M. about 4 o'clock traveled well till 6 o'clock,
when a very hard thunder storm came up and detained us *in
the road* till after eight. A thunder storm at sunset on the
Prairie is a sublime and awing scene indeed. The vivid and
forked lightning quickly succeeded by the hoarse growling
thunder impresses one most deeply of his own weakness and
the magnanimity of his God. With nothing before or near us
in sight, save the wide expanse of prairie resembling most
fully in the pale light of the moon, as she occasionally
appeared from under a murky cloud and between the vivid
lighting, the wide sea. There was no object near higher than
our own wagons, and how easy would it have been for one of
them to be struck and consume the whole crowd, for with it
was a high wind, sufficient to counteract the effects of the
drenching rain.

We traveled on till 12 o'clock and stoped near the "Pawnee
Rock"—a high mound with one side of sand stone. It derives
its name from a battle once fought there between some
company and a band of the Pawnee Indians. It has rather an
awing name, since this tribe are the most treacherous and
troublesome to the traders.

July 4th 1846. Pawnee Fork. Saturday. What a disasterous
celebration I have today. It is certainly the greatest miracle
that I have my head on my shoulders. I think I can never
forget it if I live to be as old as my grandmother.

The wagons left Pawnee Rock some time before us.—For I
was anxious to see this wonderful curiosity. We went up and
while *mi alma* with his gun and pistols kept watch, for the
wily Indian may always be apprehended here, it is a good
lurking place and they are ever ready to fall upon any
unfortunate trader behind his company—and it is necessary to

be careful, so while *mi alma* watched on the rock above and Jane stood by to watch if any should come up on the front side of me, I cut my name, among the many hundreds inscribed on the rock and many of whom I knew. It was not done well, for fear of Indians made me tremble all over and I hurried it over in any way. This I remarked would be quite an adventure to celebrate the 4th! but woe betide I have yet another to relate.

The wagons being some distance ahead we rode on quite briskly to overtake them. In an hour's time we had driven some six miles, and at *Ash creek* we came up with them. No water in the creek and the crossing pretty good only a tolerably steep bank on the first side of it, all but two had passed over, and as these were not up we drove on ahead of them to cross first. The bank though a little steep was smooth and there could be no difficulty in riding down it.—However, we had made up our minds always to walk down such places in case of accident, and before we got to it *mi alma* hallowed "woe" as he always does when he wishes to stop, but as there was no motion made by the driver to that effect, he repeated it several times and with much vehemence. We had now reached the very verge of the cliff and seeing it a good way and apparently less dangerous then jumping out as we were, he said "go on." The word was scarcely from his lips, ere we were whirled completely over with a perfect crash. One to see the wreck of that carriage now with the top and sides entirely broken to pieces, could never believe that people had come out of it alive. But strange, wonderful to say, we are almost entirely unhurt! I was considerably stunned at first and could not stand on my feet. *Mi alma* forgetting himself and entirely enlisted for my safety carried me in his arms to a shade tree, almost entirely without my knowledge, and rubbing my face and hands with whiskey soon brought me entire to myself.— My back and side are a little hurt, but is very small compared with what it might have been. *Mi alma* has his left hip and arm on which he fell both bruised and strained, but not seriously. Dear creature 'twas for me he received this, for had he not caught me in his arms as we fell he could have saved himself entirely. And then I should perhaps have been killed or much crushed for the top fell over me, and it was only his hands that kept it off of me. It is better as it is, for we can sympathise more fully with each other.

It was a perfect mess that; of people, books, bottles—one of which broke, and on my head too I believe,—guns, pistols, baskets, bags, boxes and the dear knows what else. I was insensible to it all except when something gave me a hard knock and brought me to myself. We now sought refuge in Jane's carriage for our own could only acknowledge its incapability.

By 12 o'clock we reached this place six miles, when we found all the companies which have come on before us, having been stoped by an order of Government.

Sunday 5th. I am rather better of my bruises today. It is only for a little while though, I fear; such knocks seldom hurt so much for a day or two. I am yet to suffer for it.

We are still at "The Pawnee Fork." The traders are all stoped here by an order of Government, to wait the arrival of more troops than those already ahead of us, for our protection to Santa Fe.

We are quite a respectable crowd now with some seventy-five or eighty wagons of merchandise, beside those of the soldiers. When all that are behind us come up we shall number some hundred and fifty.

And it is quite probable we shall be detained here ten days or a week at the least. I shall go regularly to housekeeping. It is quite a nice place this, notwithstanding the number of wagons and cattle we have for our near neighbours. With the great Arkansas on the South of us, the Pawnee creek to the S.W. and extensive woods in the same direction. From the west the buffalo are constantly coming in, in bands of from three or four to more than fifty.

The sight of so many military coats is quite sufficient to frighten all the Indians entirely out of the country. So we have nothing to fear either on account of starvation, thirst or sudden murder.

Monday 6th. Camp No. 26. Ours is quite the picture of a hunter's home today.

The men, most of them, have been out since sun rise, and constantly mules loaded with the spoils of their several victories, are constantly returning to camp. It is a rich sight indeed to look at the fine fat meat stretched out on ropes to dry for our sustinence when we are no longer in the region of the living animal. Such soup as we have made of the hump ribs, one of the most choice parts of the buffalo. I never eat its equal in the best hotels of N.Y. and Philad. And the sweetest butter and most delicate oil I ever tasted tis not surpassed by the marrow taken from the thigh bones.

If one cannot live and grow fat here, he must be a strange creature. Oh, how much Papa would enjoy it! He would at once acknowledge that his venison camp never equaled it.

Mi alma was out this morning on a hunt, but I sincerely hope he will never go again. I am so uneasy from the time he starts till he returns. There is danger attached to it that the excited hunter seldom thinks of till it over take him. His horse may fall and kill him; the buffalo is apt too, to whirl suddenly on his persuer, and often serious if not fatal accidents occur. It is a painful situation to be placed in, to know that the being dearest to you on earth is in momentary danger of loosing his life, or receiving for the remainder of his days, whether long or short, a tormenting wound.

The servant who was with him today, was thrown from his horse by the latter stumbling in a hole, with which the Prairies are covered, and had his head somewhat injured. And *mi alma's* horse was quite unruly.

Wednesday 8th. Camp No. 28. This is our fourth day here. It is quite a pleasant and homelike place this. They are busy in the kitchen (two wagons drawn near up and a hole dug in the ground for a fire place), preparations are making for a long jaunt on the Plains—for it seems they intend keeping us out of Santa Fe almost entirely.

The soldiers are coming in, and if we have to travel behind them, it will be poor living both for man and beast. We have all to be allowanced in our provisions from this out, or we shall have none at all.

A band of more than an hundred buffalo came almost within gun shot of the camp this morning, and for the first time I had a good opportunity of seeing the little calves. I sat down immediately and wrote to *Papa*.

Camp No. 29. Thursday 9th. We have permission today to go on as far as the ford of the Arkansas, or to Bent's Fort, as we like, and there to await the arrival of Col. Carney the commanding officer. We shall prepare to leave here tomorrow or next day.

The Fort is 180 miles, and the Ford some seventy or eighty. How long we are to be kept there, it is impossible to tell, perhaps it will be for two or three or even *six* months. Almost the length of time my *grandmother* spent in such a *palace!*

Today for the first time I have had a ride on horseback. It is a treat notwithstanding the jolting horse I was on. I am very much disappointed in my fine, noble bay. He walks and paces hard, but I must attribute it to his being spoiled in the buffalo chase. He is constantly on the lookout and requires all my strength nearly to hold him in. And I have grown to be quite an indifferent horsewoman to what I was in *my younger days!*

Friday. Camp 30th. The same routine of meat drying &c. Still lying by at Pawnee Creek—making some preparations though, to leave tomorrow. I have been sick nearly ever since

I came here the consequences of my rare celebration of the 4th I suppose.

Saturday 11th. Camp 31st. Oh how gloomy the Plains have been to me today! I am sick, rather sad feelings and everything around corresponds with them.

We have never had such a perfectly dead level before us as now. The little hillocks which formerly broke the perfectly even view have entirely disappeared. The grass is perfectly short, a real buffalo and Prairie dog and rattle snake region.

We left our camp at Pawnee Fork this morning at 9 o'clock, It is 11 o'clock and one of the warmest and most disagreeable days the Prairie ever gave birth to. We stoped as there was plenty water and the oxen tired pulling over those great steep banks. We are nooning it here.

Some twenty of the Government wagons came up. We started again at 3 o'clock and traveled on till 9½ o'clock. Stoped on the prairie with a little water though enough for the cattle, twelve miles from Pawnee creek.

All the companies are before us, or rather they have taken a new road along the River. We are to go along by ourselves across the Prairie with little wood and perhaps no water, as is most generally the case at this point of the road near the Coon Creeks and heart of the buffalo range.

Coon cr. No. 1—5 ms, from Coon Cr. No. 2. Sunday 12th. Camp 32. About 30 miles from Pawnee Fork.

The Sabbath on the Plains is not altogether without reverence. Every thing is perfectly calm. The blustering, swearing teamsters remembering the duty they owe to their Maker, have thrown aside their abusive language, and are singing the hymns perhaps that were taught by a good pious Mother. The little birds are all quiet and reverential in their songs. And nothing seems disposed to mar that calm, serene silence prevailing over the land. We have not the ringing of church bells, or the privilege of attending public worship, it is true, but we have ample time, sufficient reason &c for thinking on the great wisdom of our Creator, for praising him within ourselves for his excellent greatness in placing before us and entirely at our command so many blessings; in giving us health, minds free from care, the means of knowing and learning his wise designs. &c.

We left our camp early this morning and nooned it out on the Prairie with out more shelter from the scorching sun than that afforded by the carriage. I took so much the advantage of this as to take a quiet evening siesta of half hour. A buffalo robe spread out on the ground under the *catrin* [carriage] with the cushions for my pillow, was my whole bed, and quite an acceptable one too.

We drove on till about 12 o'clock, for the morning's drive was not a very good one, and the moon shone so bright that *mi alma* wished to drive *all* night even, and gain as much as possible, but some of the men became refractory and stubborn and stoped in the road, refusing to drive any further because it was night, notwithstanding they had driven (on account of the heat) but a short distance during the drive. So there was nothing to be done but form a corral and spend the night here. *The place is called by Mr. Gregg, Coon Creek.*

Monday 13th Noon. Big Coon Creek, No. 3. Left our last night's camp at Little Coon cr. this morning quite late, after 8 o'clock, traveled steadily on till 12 making about eight or nine miles. The day has been rather cloudy and favourable for the oxen.

Passed a great many buffalo, (some thousands) they crossed our road frequently within two or three hundred yards. They are very ugly, ill-shapen things with their long shaggy hair over their heads, and the great hump on their backs, and they look so droll running. Ring had his own fun chasing them. They draw themselves into a perfect knot switching their tails about, and throwing all feet up at once. When the dog got near to any one of them he would whirl around and commence pawing the earth with not a very friendly feeling for his delicately formed persuer, I imagine.

We have seen several antelope too this morning. It is a noble animal indeed; and there is certainly nothing that moves with more majestic pride, or with more apparent disdain to inferior animals than he does. With his proud head raised aloft, nostrels expanded wide, he moves with all the lightness, ease and grace imaginable.

And we also had a rattle-snake fracas. There were not *hundreds* killed tho', as Mr. Gregg had to do to keep his animals from suffering, but some *two* or *three* were killed in the road by our carriage driver, and these were quite enough to make me sick.

Road to Bent's Fort. Saturday 18th. Camp 38, Bank of the Arkansas. I have written nothing in my journal since Monday, and what a considerable change there has been in affairs.

Tuesday I was taken sick—and recollect that we reached the River at noon that day. Went on about six miles in the evening, struck it again about Sun down, and camped for the night. We now had in company Messrs. Harmoney, Davie, Glasgow, and two companies of soldiers' wagons. Both

Wednesday and Thursday we made pretty much the same travel, reached the crossing Thursday, when we nooned it.

Here we found it rather better to go on to the Fort especially as some two or three companies had gone before us and the Dctr. with them. Made a tolerable drive that evening, and camped on the River again. I was quite sick now took medicine.

Friday morning I was no better, and *mi alma* sẹnt a man ahead to stop the Dr. He returned in the course of four or five hours, having left the Dr. in waiting some twelve miles ahead of us.

We left camp about 2 o'clock P.M. and leaving the wagons to follow on at leisure, hurried on to this place by sun set (all the companies save Owens and our own wagons are here).

Now that I am with the Doctor I am satisfied. He is a polite delicate Frenchman (Dr. Masure) from St. Louis. He has sandy hair and whiskers, a lively address and conversation—is called an excellent physician *"especially in female cases,"* and in brevity I have great confidence in his knowledge and capacity of relieving me, though not all at once, for mine is a case to be treated gently, and slowly, a complication of diseases.

The idea of being sick on the Plains is not at all pleasant to me; it is rather terrifying than otherwise, although I have a good nurse in my servant woman Jane, and one of the kindest husbands in the world, all gentleness and affection, and would at any time suffer in my stead.

Notwithstanding the hurry in our passing them, and my sickness, I must say something of *"the Caches,"* rather a celebrated place that! They are situated about 20 miles the other side of the crossing, and are large holes dug in the ground somewhat the shape of a jug. They were made there in the winter of 1812 by a party of traders (Beard and others) who were overtaken by a severe winter, their animals died, and these pits called "Caches," a word of French origin, were made, the insides lined with moss and whatever else of the kind they could obtain, and their goods concealed in them till the following spring, when after procuring more assistance, they removed them. They are situated about a quarter of a mile from the River, on rather an elevated piece of ground, and within a hundred yards of the road, which runs at present between them and the river. They are quite as noted as any point on the road and few travellers pass without visiting them. I was rather too much of an invalid, though, to go nearer than the road.

Part III
Pictorial Journey

Artists

A VARIETY OF ARTISTS' works are used in this section. However, the three artists whose works are most frequently represented in this section are Josiah Gregg, Lieutenant James Abert, and Ben Wittick. Gregg's works date from the 1830s and early 1840s during the Mexican era. Abert's represent the mid-1840s during the transitional period when the United States took possession of Santa Fe. Wittick's photographs are from the late 1870s and 1880s. In addition, there are numerous other individual items from a variety of recorders. The recent photographs that accompany the early items were taken by the author on his various trips along the Santa Fe Trail.

Josiah Gregg as a young man suffered from poor health. As he wrote, his physicians finally suggested that he ". . . take a trip across the Prairies, and, in the change of air and habits . . . to seek the health that their science had failed to bestow." He joined an ox wagon company and headed for Santa Fe and never regretted their advice. He wrote, "The effects of this journey were in the first place to re-establish my health, and, in the second, to beget a passion for the Prairie life which I never expect to survive." His record of his years engaged in the Santa Fe trade, 1831–1843, appeared as *Commerce Of The Prairies*. His record of his eight crossings to Santa Fe is included in his work. The engravings or drawings included here are taken from his book.

Lieutenant James W. Abert graduated from the United States Military Academy in 1842 at the age of twenty-two. The following year he joined the Topographical Engineers. He served under Fremont in 1845 during Fremont's third exploring expedition to the West. He was detached in command of an expedition to survey the Canadian River. In 1846, he joined General Kearny's "Army of the West" that invaded the Southwest and then surveyed the new possessions. Both these two assignments became the source of his works used herein. He made numerous pen/pencil drawings and water colors of plants, animals, Indians, and sites encountered on his two western survey assignments. He served in a variety of places after his assignment in New Mexico including several located in Europe. He then served in the Civil War and as a result of poor health and injuries, he resigned in 1864. He died in 1897. His works recorded in different Congressional reports provided insights into the newly acquired lands of New Mexico and the Southwest.

Ben Wittick was one of the earlier photographers of the Southwest. Much of his work is now in the possession of the Museum of New Mexico. He moved to Santa Fe about 1878 and took photos for the Atchison, Topeka, and Santa Fe Railroad. His career started during the last years of the Santa Fe Trail and continued during the latter part of the nineteenth century. He is best known for his photos of the railroad's construction and the various Indian groups of New Mexico and Arizona. He died of a snake bite from a snake which was to be a gift to the Hopi Indian Snake Dancers in 1903.

Come travel along the Santa Fe now, and see the trail as depicted by our early recorders, and compare them with the trail today.

SANTA FE SPRING

The Big Spring, or Santa Fe Spring, is located below Arrow Rock near the landing at the crossing of the Missouri. The spring was a natural gathering place for Santa Fe traders who would fill their water barrels before heading up the bank from the river landing.

ARROW ROCK TAVERN

Joseph Huston, one of the commissioners who laid out Arrow Rock, built this tavern in 1834. During its early days many famous people, including Thomas Benton and Kit Carson, visited the tavern. Today, you can dine as they did more than a century and a half ago.

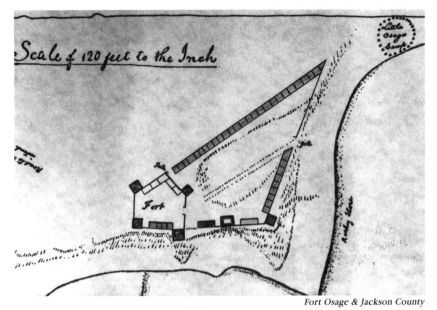

Fort Osage & Jackson County

FORT OSAGE

This plan of the original layout of the fort was drawn by William Clark, of the famous Lewis and Clark expedition of the Louisiana Purchase. Construction was started in 1808 and the fort was finally abandoned in 1827. It was the first American outpost constructed in the newly acquired Louisiana Territory. Part of the fort has been reconstructed on the original foundations according to plans which are in possession of the War Department.

FORT OSAGE TODAY

This view is from one of the blockhouses looking west towards another blockhouse and the barracks. This corresponds to the lowest block on the drawing above. Unfortunately, no drawings other than the one of the layout of the fort are known to exist. For those visiting the fort, the twentieth century is left behind and the era of the early fur trappers and traders is entered.

Kansas State Historical Society

FORT LEAVENWORTH DRAWING

This drawing of Fort Leavenworth probably dates from around the late 1840s to the early 1850s. The artist is unknown. Notice the blockhouse and the trail coming up from the river landing. The military function of the fort was to protect the growing Santa Fe trade. Later as the trails to Oregon, Utah, and California developed, Fort Leavenworth also served as a jumping off place for emigrants. James Wilkins, an artist traveling to California in 1849 made a drawing looking up at the fort from the base of the hill to the right where the riverboats landed.

FORT LEAVENWORTH TODAY

The stone wall shown on the left side of the photo appears to be all that remains from the old blockhouse depicted in the old painting. The site is located at the intersection of Kearny Avenue, Scott Avenue, and Riverside Drive. Scott Avenue runs north through what was the backyards of the buildings in the painting. Today, additional buildings flank each side of the roads and block most of the view of the river.

FORT LEAVENWORTH — THE ROOKERY

The Rookery was built in 1832 and is the oldest building at Fort Leavenworth. It is located on the eastern side of the square and Parade Grounds. The rear of the building and backyard is shown in the old painting. The Rookery still serves as living quarters for soldiers. The fort was founded in 1827 on the banks overlooking the Missouri River and replaced Fort Osage for the military. Francis Parkman wrote in 1846, "Fort Leavenworth is in fact no fort, being without defense works, except two blockhouses . . . . In the square grassy area, surrounded by barracks and the quarters of the officers, the men were passing and repassing, or lounging among the trees." Today visitors can also walk and lounge among the trees.

FORT LEAVENWORTH — SANTA FE TRAIL RUTS

This shows part of the old landing area. Today the river no longer cuts close to the bluff. Note the deep swale going up the hill in the center. Supplies and wagons were off-loaded from river steamers that stopped here. This was the beginning of the trail from Fort Leavenworth. The blockhouse was located at the top of the hill where the trail came up from the river.

National Park Service

WESTPORT LANDING
William Henry Jackson saw Westport Landing more than twenty years after its development as a trailhead. By then the area had been built up. Here is his vision of what it might have looked like in its earlier years.

WESTPORT LANDING TODAY
Here is a view of the area today. Jackson would have difficulty recognizing it.

Kansas State Historical Society

INDEPENDENCE SQUARE

The present-day Independence Courthouse is located in the old town square that was depicted in Charles Dana's *The United States Illustrated* in the 1850s. This square has often been referred to as the beginning of the Santa Fe, Oregon, and California Trails. Wagon trains were reported to have lined up and started their journey west from here. In May of 1846 Edwin Bryant noted, "It has been for some years the principal outfitting point for the Santa Fe traders, and will probably so continue. Many of the houses around the public square are constructed of brick, but the majority of the buildings are frames . . . . Long trains of oxen, sometimes as many as ten or fifteen yokes, strung together pulling huge tented wagons, designed for some Santa Fe trading expedition, were moving about the streets, under the direction of numerous drivers, cracking their whips and making a great noise." Within a short distance of this square are many sites associated with western history.

INDEPENDENCE SQUARE TODAY

Today the courthouse is much larger than shown above. It is said to contain remnants of the 1846 courthouse. As in the past the square is still a hub of activity. This site also seems to have been the location chosen by James Shepherd for his farm or plantation before the site was chosen for the county seat of Jackson County. He moved about a half mile southeast of the square. Some early Santa Fe travelers mention the Shepherd farm.

INDEPENDENCE SPRING & CABIN

In 1827, the same year in which the U.S. Army started constructing Fort Leavenworth, the town of Independence was built. The site was selected because of the area's many fine springs and woods. The Brady cabin, one of the oldest structures in Independence, is thought to have been built in 1836. It was moved to this park which also has a reconstructed spring. The spring was originally located on the hill to the west of it. The spring was mentioned by Sibley during the 1826 survey. The cabin itself has an interesting history because of its ties with the Younger family.

BRADY CABIN TODAY

INDEPENDENCE LOG COURTHOUSE

This is a photo of the original 1827 log courthouse. It has been moved to its present site; as is readily noticeable, its front has also been altered somewhat since its construction. The logs for this structure were cut by James Shepherd's slave Sam.

ALEXANDER MAJORS' HOME

Alexander Majors started his freighting business along the Santa Fe Trail in 1848. With his partners, Waddell and Russell, they soon became one of the major freighting companies of the West. He built this house in 1856 on a hill overlooking the surrounding countryside. Today it has been refurbished to represent its early period.

NATIONAL FRONTIER TRAILS CENTER

Here is the new National Frontier Trails Center. It is situated on the location of the Waggoner-Gates Mill site. This was also the location of one of the famous springs of Independence, and later the first mill was established here in 1847 by John Overfelt. The mill was purchased by Peter Waggoner in 1866 and expanded. It became the home of the "Queen of the Pantry Flour." Today part of the old mill building has been incorporated into the trails center museum. On the hill across the street is the Bingham-Waggoner home which has been restored.

SHAWNEE MISSION TODAY

One of the major places mentioned by people heading west was the Shawnee Methodist Mission. The Kansas State Historical Society has restored the mission and three of the early buildings constructed between 1839 and 1845 are open to visitors. This was the last touch with civilization that many emigrants were to have before embarking on many months of hard travel. Both the famous and the common stopped here. Pierson Barton Reading wrote on May 20, 1843, "Visited the Shawnee Mission under charge of Reverend Mr. Berryman. This is a Methodist Mission and appears to be doing much for the benefit of the Shawnees . . . . The improvements are two big brick buildings with a large barn, stables, wheelwrite, blacksmith and shoemakers. The school consists at present of about one hundred scholars; 40 females and 60 males." Ten years later another emigrant Celinda E. Hines wrote on April 19, 1853, "The farm consists of about six hundred acres. There are three large brick buildings. We went to the female department and saw forty Indian girls in school . . . . The mission is beautifully situated."

MINOR PARK SWALE

The first major stream crossing made by the traders and emigrants after leaving Independence was over the Blue River near the present-day Red Bridge. Just after the crossing, they made a pull up the hill to the prairie. Through Minor Park Santa Fe traders, and other emigrants all passed. Their numbers and the weight of their wagons left numerous deep swales in the hillside. Edwin Bryant, one of those emigrants, wrote on May 6, 1846, "At 9 o'clock we resumed our march. Fording the creek (Blue River), and crossing the timbered bottom of the stream over a very deep and muddy road, we entered another magnificent prairie beyond the Missouri line and within the Indian territory." Susan Magoffin also appears to have crossed there before turning off to camp nearby at Fitzhugh's Mill. She also noted that the area was comprised of "thick wood of oaks and scrubby underbrush" situated at the beginning of the prairie.

This is the hill Bryant and others climbed after fording the river and crossing the wooded bottom. Today a picnic area is located in the wooded bottomlands. In the neighboring Minor Park, one can walk up the hill in the deep swales made by all those who headed down the Santa Fe Trail.

ROLLING PRAIRIE

One of the most memorable experiences mentioned by the emigrants was the first view of the rolling prairie lands of what is now Kansas.

On May 6, 1846, Edwin Bryant wrote, "As we approached what is called the Blue Prairie, the road became much drier and less difficult. The vast prairie itself soon opened before us in all its grandeur and beauty. I had never before beheld extensive scenery of this kind. The many descriptions of the prairies of the west had forestalled in some measure the first impressions produced by the magnificent landscape that lay spread out before me as far as the eye could reach, bounded alone by the blue wall of the sky. No description, however, which I have read of these scenes, or which can be written, can convey more than a faint impression of the imagination of their effects upon the eye. The view of the illimitable succession of great undulations and flowery slopes, of every gentle and graceful configuration, stretching away and away, until they fade from the sight in the dim distance, creates a wild and scarely controllable ecstasy of admiration."

Two days later Bryant was still enthralled by the prairie. On May 8, 1846, Bryant wrote, "It is impossible for me to convey to the reader the impressions made upon my mind by the survey of these measureless and undulating plains, with their ground of the freshest verdue, and their garniture of flame-like flowers decorating every slope and hilltop. It would seem as if here the Almighty had erected a finished abode for his rational creatures, and ornamented it with beauties of landscape and exuberance and variety of production far above our feeble conceptions or efforts at imitation."

COUNCIL OAK TODAY — COUNCIL GROVE

On August 5, 1825, George Sibley wrote, ". . . arrived at Breakfast at the Main Branch of The Nee Ozho River; and here we find most excellent pasturage, and a Large & beautiful Grove of fine Timber . . . . As we propose to Meet the Osage Chiefs in council Here, to negotiate a Treaty with them for the Road &c. I suggested the propriety of naming the place "Council Grove" which was agreed to, & Capt. Cooper directed to Select a Suitable Tree, & to record this name in Strong and durable characters—which was done."

Today, all that is left of the great White Oak on which John Walker carved the name, date, and mileage to Fort Osage, is its trunk, and that is protected from the elements by the covering shown in the picture.

Kansas State Historical Society

CONN STORE — COUNCIL GROVE

This early photo of the Conn store was probably taken in the late 1860s after it had been sold to Shamleffer and James. The "Stone Store" was built in 1858 by Malcolm Conn in partnership with Thomas Hill and James Munkres. Conn advertised, "He will be undrsold [sic] by none" "HE CAN AND WILL SELL GOODS CHEAPER THAN ANY OTHER FIRM IN SOUTH WESTERN KANSAS. HE FEARS NO COMPETITION." This store and the Hays store were the last major source of supplies for those heading further down the Trail.

CONN STORE TODAY

Today the Conn Store still stands on the same corner. Its name has changed and it has been altered some and enlarged, but much of the structure is still intact. The Hays store located down the street also stands today but has been altered considerably.

KAW MISSION TODAY

This school was built in 1850 for the Indian children. By 1854, it was the school for the white children of Council Grove, and at times, it also served as lodgings for those traveling on the Santa Fe Trail.

LAST CHANCE STORE TODAY

This small store was established by Thomas Hill in 1859 after he sold his interest in the Conn store. As can be seen, it was much smaller than the Conn Store and was never as important. It still stands on its original location and is open to the public on a limited basis. It is no longer on the hot open prairie, but is shaded by large cool trees.

Museum of New Mexico

COW CREEK

This old photo, which probably dates from the late 1860s, shows Buffalo Bill Mathewson's well and the Cow Creek army station at the crossing of Cow Creek. On July 1, 1846, Susan Magoffin noted, "The crossing here is very bad and took us till moon down to cross." Josiah Gregg wrote, "Next day we reached Cow Creek, where all the difficulties encountered at the Little Arkansas had to be reconquered: but after digging, bridging, shouldering the wheels, with the usual accompaniment of whooping, swearing and cracking of whips, we soon got safely across and encamped in the valley beyond."

COW CREEK TODAY

Today there is a small rest stop at the former Cow Creek Station and a cover over Buffalo Bill's well. A bridge crosses the creek just north of the old fording area.

Kansas State Historical Society

PAWNEE ROCK

This drawing by Ado Hunnius was made in 1867. It shows as Pawnee Rock as it appeared to the early traders before the area was settled and the rock used as a source of building materials. (See also the diary section.)

George Sibley wrote on August 30, 1825, "We first rode . . . to a remarkable Rocky Point which projects into the Bottom from a High Ridge; these rocks are very large and of a glossy Black colour; Towards the River, the face is nearly perpendicular. We rode to the top which is probably 50 feet above the plain below, and from whence there is a charming view of the country in every direction."

Matt Field who visited the rock in 1839 wrote, "Pawnee Rock springs like a hugh wart from the carpeted green of the prairie . . . . One tall, rugged portion of it is rifted from the main mass of rock, and stands totally inaccessible and alone. Some twenty names are cut in stone, and the dates are marked as far as ten years back."

"Leaving the wagons behind, our small crowd of leisure travellers rode forward to view the Rock. At the base we released our animals from their trappings, and haltered them to the tough roots of clustering plum trees, leaving them to graze while we sought around for an accessible pathway to the summit. This we reached with slight difficulty in clambering, a few scratched knuckles, and our pockets full of cold buffalo meat. Here we seated ourselves upon the rock for a jollification. We killed one rattlesnake and drove away half a dozen others, after which we quietly laid in our preemption right to the territory. From the eminence we glanced around the prospect, munching our cold luncheon with as much pure exhilaration and pleasure as ever was known by the most systematic gourmand seated at a groaning table of viands. Health and hunger are far more luxurious condiments than any French culinary artiste has ever yet invented, and our banqueting hall was of dimensions and beauty that art can never imitate without being lost forever."

Santa Fe Trail Center Museum

EARLY PHOTO OF PAWNEE ROCK
This early photo, taken at the turn of the century, shows a view without trees.

PAWNEE ROCK TODAY
Today trees block the view of Pawnee Rock as one approaches it from a distance, and a portion of the rock has been carted off. However, one can still climb up the face of the rock, eat a picnic lunch, and climb the viewing tower to survey the surrounding area much as Matt Field, Susan Magoffin and other earlier travelers did. Fortunately, there are no rattlesnakes around today to worry about. The names of the early travelers are all gone, only those from this past century can still be found.

Museum of New Mexico, Neg. No. 87450

INDIAN LOOKOUT

The drawing above appears to have been based on the view from Pawnee Rock looking down at the surrounding area. Note the wagon formation here is the same as used in Gregg's drawings in his *Commerce Of The Prairies*.

PAWNEE ROCK VIEW TODAY

DEAD BUFFALOES.

Harper's Magazine

PAWNEE FORK

On George Brewerton's return to Independence the party he traveled with broke a cardinal rule of trail travel, that you should always cross the creek before you camp. His party camped before crossing and when they awoke, the Pawnee Fork was swollen from prairie thunderstorms. They could not ford so he took a walk along the banks. The river he saw was full of buffalo carcasses that had drowned after being stuck in the mud.

PAWNEE FORK TODAY

This is how the Pawnee Fork looked recently, swollen and muddy after some long and violent prairie thunderstorms. There are no buffalos in the area today.

FORT LARNED — OLDEST PHOTO

This is the earliest photo. It was taken in 1869 and shows the construction of the stone buildings that replaced the adobe buildings of the earlier Fort Larned. At the time this was taken the construction was still in process. It was taken from the old ox-bow of the Pawnee Fork to the east of the fort just behind the present commissary storehouse. The commanding officer's quarters is located directly behind the flagpole.

FORT LARNED TODAY

Because of the growth of trees and the construction of the commissary storehouse it is impossible to duplicate the old photo.

National Park Service, Fort Larned

FORT LARNED — JUNIOR OFFICERS' QUARTERS

This old photo shows the southernmost of the two junior officers' quarters. This is the same building that is just to the left of center in the old photo of Fort Larned. Note that the porch has been added. It probably dates from the 1870s.

FORT LARNED — JUNIOR OFFICERS' QUARTERS TODAY

Today, the building has been restored and appears much the same. However, trees now shade much of the area.

Daughters of the Army Collection, U.S. Army Military History Institute
FORT LARNED — COMMANDING OFFICER'S QUARTERS
Here is the Commanding Officer's Quarters as it looked in 1870s. Today, the inside
has been refurbished, and from the photo below, it seems as though an old soldier
would still feel right at home today. He would certainly enjoy the shade provided by
the trees from the hot Kansas sun.

FORT LARNED — COMMANDING OFFICER'S QUARTERS TODAY

Gregg, COMMERCE OF THE PRAIRIES

PRAIRIE DOG TOWN

The prairie dog town was one of the sights often seen and mentioned by many of the travelers. George Sibley wrote on August 23, 1825, "I also saw some Killdeers, and a small species of Hawk that is peculiar to the Dog Towns in which they reside. In one of those Towns I saw several large Rattlesnakes. I spent nearly an Hour in one of them, which is more than a league Square, I think, observing its curious Inhabitants. The Prairie Dog, as it is called from its barking like a Puppy, is about the size & colour of a Rabbit but resembles more the Grey Squirrel in other particulars. It burrows in the ground to a great depth, lives on grass, and in pairs. They are very wild and difficult to catch or kill, Tho' I made out to shoot one this morning. What is curious is that the Dogs, Snakes, & Hawks all occupy the same dens—at least I have frequently seen them all run into the same Holes. How they agree together I cannot tell." Gregg devotes three pages to them and Susan Magoffin's description of a dog town is included in the diary section.

Harper's Magazine

PRAIRIE DOG TOWN
Here is a similar scene made by George Brewerton in 1848.

PRAIRIE DOG TOWN TODAY

This prairie dog town is found in the Fort Larned detached site and is located right along the wide swales of the Santa Fe Tail. While it is not as large as the one Sibley and Gregg encountered, one can easily spend an hour trying to get a good close look at the prairie dogs there. They tend to hide when you get too close. For those who drive out to the site of Bent's New Fort, there is a prairie dog town more than a mile long.

Kansas State Historical Society

FORT DODGE

Fort Dodge was built in 1864 near the junction of the wet and dry routes of the Santa Fe Trail and between the Lower Crossing and Middle Crossings of the Arkansas. This view is from the Santa Fe Trail and the northeast corner of the fort. The commanding officer's quarters is the second building from the left, and the Pershing Barracks is the long low building on the right.

FORT DODGE TODAY

Fort Dodge is now a Kansas State Soldiers Home. Trees and other subsequently built structures now block the view seen above. This is a close-up view of the Pershing Barracks which was built in 1867. It is the same as the long low building in the old photo.

Abert's Journal, THROUGH THE COUNTRY OF THE COMANCHE INDIANS.
Copyright 1970, John Howell Books

BUFFALO

While buffalo were sometimes encountered in eastern Kansas, it was along the Arkansas that most travelers encountered them. Travelers eagerly looked for them and frequently chased and hunted them. Depending on the year, buffalo sightings numbered from one to several thousand. The painting was made by Lt. Abert. Gregg devotes many pages in his book to the buffalo, sightings, the hunting of them, and the various uses for them.

BUFFALO TODAY

This photo shows a bull from the buffalo herd located in the State Buffalo Preserve described in the Museum Section. Even today, seeing buffalo roaming on the plains stirs both one's blood and imagination. In 1848 George Brewerton wrote, "The Buffalo, the universal theme of prairie travel are to be found at times in such immense herds that their hugh forms darken the plains as far as the eye can reach, while the very earth seems trembling beneath the shock of their trampling hoofs, as they rend the air with deep mouthed bellowing."

From MEMOIRS OF MY LIFE, by John C. Fremont or National Archives

BIG TIMBER

Big Timber was like an oasis spot on the treeless prairie and trail. It was a narrow strip of large cottonwood trees along the valley of the Arkansas River from Big Sandy Creek to Caddo (Caddoa) Creek. At times it served as a favorite campground for the Indians. Bent also built his new fort here, and, later, the army built old Fort Lyon. Matt Field wrote, "When exhausted beneath the blazing heat of the prairies, the old travellers would tell us of Big Timber, of the ancient trees, the cool stream, the gushing spring . . . ." He continued to describe it, "Here the expedition with which we released horses and mules from harness and turned them loose upon the rich grass, and flung ourselves, some into the stream, some beneath the trees for slumber, displayed an alacrity surpising after our long hardship. Vast sunflower beds spread far and near around the spot, and tall carpets of juicy grass contrasted their emerald hue with the bright yellow of the sun-worshippers. A thick forest of venerable trees sheltered us from the heat, and beneath them wandered a stream yet cool with mountain snow. From the bank a spring gushed, shooting its crystal water far across the hurryint tide of this young tributary to the Arkansas. We saw the wild deer bounding from shore to shore and scarcely wetting a foot; and among the sunflower beds the hugh back of a buffalo here and there was seen, as the ponderous brute broke down the stalks before him while pressing forward to a fresher pasture ground."

BIG TIMBER TODAY

Today, Big Timber has changed considerably. Even by 1850, the big trees were being cut and many of the wild animals had disappeared. Today, the town of Lamar, Colorado is located on the south bank of the Arkansas of what was once a paradise on the prairie. Trees grow along the immediate river bank and on the islands, but the large cool forest is now gone.

Abert's Journal, THROUGH THE COUNTRY OF THE COMANCHE INDIANS.
Copyright 1970, John Howell Books

BENT'S FORT — EXTERIOR

This is the fort that served as the center of the Bents' trading empire. It was a major stopping point for caravans along the Mountain Route and the center of civilization for travelers. It even had a billards room. General Kearny stopped here as did Susan Magoffin.

BENT'S FORT — EXTERIOR TODAY

Today the fort appears much the way it did to the Santa Fe traders as they appraoched it. The National Park's meticulous reproduction of Bent's Fort, both inside and outside, would make even Lt. Abert feel at home.

Abert

BENT'S FORT — EXTERIOR

Above is the drawing by Abert of the exterior of Bent's Fort. This is better known than his painting. Below is a view from a different angle. It was used to illustrate Doniphan's Expedition. Abert's proportions are more accurate.

BENT'S FORT — EXTERIOR

Doniphan

BENT'S FORT TODAY

Here are views of Bent's Fort similar to those by Abert and Doniphan.

BENT'S FORT TODAY

Abert's Journal, THROUGH THE COUNTRY OF THE COMANCHE INDIANS.
Copyright 1970, John Howell Books

BENT'S FORT — INTERIOR

Lt. J. W. Abert first visited the fort during his trip in 1845 as a member of Fremont's third exploring expedition. He visited the fort again in 1846-7 and returned over the Santa Fe Trail. He painted both the exterior and interior. In his interior painting of Bent's Fort made on August 7, 1845, Abert shows some Cheyenne Indians sitting and others dancing celebrating their vistory over the Pawnee.

BENT'S FORT — INTERIOR TODAY

If you close your eyes and stand quietly inside the fort, you can almost hear the Indian celebration in the wind.

SPANISH PEAKS

Here are the famous Spanish Peaks, the Wah-To-Yah, or Breasts of the World used to illustrate Fremont's *Memoirs Of My Life*. They served as a landmark for the travelers west of Bent's Fort along the Timpas Creek as the trail turned to approach the Raton Mountains. The last view travelers would have of them was for a brief instant at the top of Raton Pass when the trail made a short jog north before turning south again and down the other side of the mountain.

SPANISH PEAKS TODAY

National Archives

SPANISH PEAKS

Abert made this painting just southwest of the present town of Hoehne, Colorado. It was in sight of these peaks that William Bent befriended two Cheyennes. He placed his own life in danger of attack by the Comanches under Bull Hump while protecting the two Cheyennes. However, this act of friendship was the beginning of the strong ties between the Bents and the Cheyennes and helped to make the Bents' trading empire possible.

SPANISH PEAKS TODAY

Western History Collection, Denver Public Library
RATON MOUNTAINS

The climb over the Raton Mountains was hard and dangerous. Susan Magoffin, like many others took five days to accomplish it in 1846. On August 15, 1846, she wrote, "Still in the Raton, traveling on the rate of half mile an hour, with the road growing worse and worse. I have scarcely ventured in the carriage this morning; but have "climbed the hills" not on my own feet as I did yesterday, but on the back of my caballo (horse) . . . . Worse and worse the road! They are even taking the mules from the carriages this P.M. and as half dozen men by bodily exertions are pulling them down the hills. And it take a dozen men to steady a wagon with all its wheels locked—and for one who is some distance off to hear the crash it makes over the stones, is truly alarming . . . . We came to camp about half an hour after dusk, having accomplished the great travel of six or eight hundred yards during the day." Later, once Dick Wootton's Toll Road was built over the Raton, travel was much easier and faster.

Matt Field wrote, ". . . we were obliged to follow the wandering of a clear, pebble-paved stream, called the Ratone; and sometimes where cliff and precipice utterly barred our way, the wagons were obliged to be drawn along the bed of the creek. At one place, so difficult was our progress, that we advanced but a mile and a half in a day. Overhanding branches and projecting roots were obliged to be cut away, and heavy rock removed, for the creek was barely wide enough to admit the wagons between the rugged banks."

RATON TODAY

Construction of the railroad and the recent Interstate Highway has greatly altered much of the streambed and the route over the mountains. However, the trail at this curve along the mountainside appears to be very similar to the drawing on the previous page. Since this photo was taken, this area has been graded and altered somewhat.

Western History Collection, Denver Public Library

RATON ZIGZAG

The Atchison, Topeka, & Santa Fe Railroad first climbed over the Raton Mountain by a series of switch-backs. Later a tunnel was built through the mountain and the route over it was abandoned. However, even today the scars left by the zigzags are still evident.

RATON TODAY

This view is similar to the drawing above. It was taken from the rest stop at the top of Raton Pass going south on I-25.

FORDING THE ARKANSAS.

Harper's Magazine

CROSSING THE ARKANSAS

This is a view of a caravan at the crossing of the Arkansas River. In 1844 James Webb described the crossing. "We found the river in fair fordable condition and crossed in one day by double teams, with twelve yoke of oxen to each wagon, with three or four drivers to a wagon, and plenty of men to walk beside the wagon to lift at the sides in case of danger of turning over, or to roll the wheels in case of miring down. The current is so rapid and the quicksand so treacherous that a wagon shakes and rattles by the sand washing from under the wheels as much as it would going over the worst coblestone pavement. And if the team stops for a very few minutes, it will settle so deep that it is with the greatest difficulty it can be got out."

ARKANSAS RIVER TODAY

This is a view of the Arkansas River near the Middle Crossing. The sandy bottom of the river is clearly evident. However, irrigation has taken its toll, and the river runs almost dry in many areas throughout much of the area during the summer.

Kansas State Historical Society

FORDING THE ARKANSAS
While this early photo shows a fording of the Arkansas, it is not on the Santa Fe Trail itself, but near Great Bend. However, it must be very similar to what the ford was like further up the Arkansas.

THE ARKANSAS TODAY

A SHOT AT THE COMANCHES.

Harper's Magazine

INDIANS ON THE ARKANSAS

George Brewerton, returning from California and Santa Fe encountered Comanches at the crossing of the Arkansas in 1848 after crossing the Jornada. This is his drawing of the incident. Below is a similar view. Note the tall phragmites Brewerton used for cover. Today, the author could find them at only one of the middle crossings of the Arkansas.

ARKANSAS TODAY

Gregg, COMMERCE OF THE PRAIRIES
INDIAN ALARM ON THE CIMARRON RIVER
On June 19, 1831 as Gregg's caravan crossed the Jornada and approached what they thought was Sand Creek (but in reality was the Cimarron), they encountered Indians. On a hillside overlooking the valley the caravan took their defensive position. Fortunately, the Indians were with their families and were peaceful.

CIMARRON VALLEY TODAY
Below is a similar view from a hillside overlooking the valley of the Cimarron near where Gregg's caravan probably would have mistaken the Cimarron valley for the Sand Creek Valley.

WAGON BED SPRINGS TODAY

This is the famous Lower Cimarron Spring, later known as the Wagon Bed Spring, that was like a pinpoint on the bank of the Cimarron River and the goal of the caravans crossing the dreaded Jornada. This is what Jedediah Smith was looking for when he was killed.

AUTOGRAPH ROCK

As found on the other major trails west, travelers frequently carved their names into rocks and cliffs along the way. This picture is of a cliff a few miles west of Upper or Flag Spring. Note the Hispanic name reflecting the dominance of Mexican traders on the route. The Delgado family was well-known along the trail.

McNEES CROSSING TODAY

This is the crossing named after the two traders, McNees and Monroe who were shot by Indians there in 1828. It is also the location where Josiah Gregg celebrated Independence Day on July 4, 1831.

RABBIT EARS TODAY

This was another of the famous landmarks along the Santa Fe Trail. The landscape in the area has not changed much since the traders passed. The name does not reflect the shape of the hills. It was the name of an Indian chief who lived in the area.

APPROACHING ROUND MOUND

This view of Round Mound shows how it rises from the plains. Little appears to have changed in the area. Gregg climbed the mound. His drawing seems to have been made from halfway up the ridge of rocks running up to the right of center.

ROUND MOUND VIEW

Here is Gregg's view from Round Mound. Gregg writes, "As the caravan was passing under the northern base of the Round Mound, it presented a very fine and imposing spectacle to those who were upon its summit. The wagons marched slowly in four parallel columns, but in broken lines, often at intervals of many rods between. The unceasing 'crack, crack,' of the wagoner's whips, resembling the frequent reports of distant guns, almost make one believe that a skirmish was actually taking place between two parties . . . . As our camp was pitched but a mile west of Round Mount, those who lingered upon its summit could have an interesting view of the evolutions of 'forming' the wagons . . . ."

Gregg, COMMERCE OF THE PRAIRIES

The view from the top of Round Mound is spectacular, but the wind blows constantly. Get permission and be careful climbing, for you will not be the only one on the Mound. The author came across two rattlesnakes. Gregg's camp would have been on the left side of the photo above.

ROCK CROSSING CANADIAN TODAY
This is the "El Vedo de las Piedras" or the stony ford of the Canadian River. Here the caravans found a safe and solid footing for the wagons. North of this crossing the river bed is extremely sandy, and to the south is the deep Canadian Canyon. Many a wagon crossed here and left scars on both the rocks and the land.

Livery Stable Antiques

LIVERY STABLE

While the town of Springer was not located on the old Santa Fe Trail, it was located by the tracks of the Atchison, Topeka, & Santa Fe Railroad which replaced the old Santa Fe Trail.

This livery stable was built during the last year of the old trail.

LIVERY STABLE TODAY

Today it looks much the same as it did in 1880 with the exception of the big trees which now shade the area. Inside it is a shop that is an antique lover's delight. It offers a wide variety of items for sale. Ask the dealers to tell you some of the interesting tales about the town, outlaws, and the stable.

WAGON MOUND TODAY

This is the last of the famous landmarks on the Cimarron Cutoff. It was in view of the traders for about three days as they approached. It was also the site of the Mail Coach attack of 1850.

TRAIL RUTS TODAY

These are the remnants of the trail as it approached the area near Fort Union. The modern Interstate parallels them as it appraoches Fort Union, Watrous, and the Sapello River.

OLD FORT UNION
This drawing of the first Fort Union was made by Joseph Heger in 1859. It was made from a point about two-thirds of the way up the mesa to the west of the fort. The later fort was situated in the center of the plains.

OLD FORT UNION — VIEW TODAY

Today trees and brush have grown up to block some of the view and the large boulders in the drawing. However the swales left from the old roads are still evident in the plain below. The stone foundation and chimney bases of the commanding officer's quarters can be seen in this photo. The adobe ruins are not from the first Fort Union, but from the arsenal of the third Fort Union whose ruins lie to the right of center out in the distant plain.

G.S.A. — National Archives and Record Service

MECHANICS' CORRAL

This old photo above shows the Mechanics' Corral in the 1870s from a point looking generally towards the southeast. The photo below also shows the Mechanics' Corral as it appeared in September of 1866 shortly after it was built. It was also taken looking generally towards the southeast. Both were taken from the roof looking into the corral. Note the trees that were planted in the earlier photo, but not present in the later one. Perhaps the trees perished because it was too dry, or they were removed for additional space in the corral.

U.S. Signal Corps Photo, National Archives

MECHANICS' CORRAL TODAY

Fort Union has weathered greatly since the old photos were taken. However, one can still get a feel of the activity that must have occurred here when the fort was very busy.

U.S. Signal Corps Photo, National Archives
FORT UNION OFFICERS' ROW PHOTO
This photo shows the officers' quarters as it looked in the 1870s. Today only the rock
chimneys and some of the adobe remnants of those fine old buildlings remain.

FORT UNION OFFICERS' ROW TODAY

EFFECT OF THE MIRAGE—"FALSE PONDS."

Harper's Magazine

PRAIRIE

For eastbound wagon caravans, the area between Las Vegas and La Junta (Watrous) was the first contact with the prairie. The Mora River flows in the area, and as a result, the area was sometimes referred to as the Mora. This area was used by the eastbound caravans as an organizational point similar to that played by Council Grove for the westbound caravans. These lithographs are based on drawings by George Brewerton. Like westbound travelers, he was awed by his first view of the prairie. The drawing above shows mirages on the vast prairie, while the lower one shows a whirlwind with a westbound caravan approaching what appears to be the Las Vegas area.

Harper's Magazine

WHIRLWIND ON THE PRAIRIES.

PRAIRIE TODAY

Here is a view of the sea of grasses that the modern traveler can still see a few miles east of Las Vegas. Unfortunately, the author did not experience any mirages nor any whirlwinds in the area. Both pictures were just off I-25 only a couple of miles apart. The top picture looks east, while the bottom picture looks west.

Aberts A Report and Map of the Examination of New Mexico

SAN MIGUEL DEL VADO

This copy of a lithograph of the town of San Miguel was based on a drawing by Lt. Abert. The original drawing appears to have been made from a small hill east of the Pecos River where the trail forded the river to enter San Miguel. On September 25 Lt. Abert wrote, "In the evening we made a visit to the village. Here is a good-sized church, built somewhat after the style of the cathedrals in the Old Country. I made a distant sketch of the town and then a nigh one of the church. The whole structure is of adobes."

Josiah Gregg wrote, ". . . we entered San Miquel, the first settlement of note upon our route. This consists of irregular clusters of mud-wall huts, and is situated in the fertile valley of Rio Pecos . . ." San Miguel was the port of entry for the early traders.

SAN MIGUEL TODAY

Today the town is hidden behind the trees that have grown up along the Pecos River. The old Santa Fe Trail came right through the town. Today, however, the main Interstate highway to Santa Fe lies two miles to the north of the town.

Western America in 1846-47: The Original Travel Diary of Lieutenant J.W. Abert,
Ed. John Galvin, John Howell Books

SAN MIGUEL CHURCH

Here is the church that the Santa Fe traders saw when they crossed the Pecos River.
This was also the first Mexican town that the early traders encountered. This is a
copy of Abert's 1846 watercolor. Susan Magoffin noted that, "The village of San
Miguel is both larger and cleaner than any we have passed; it has a church, and a
public square, neither of which are in the others."

SAN MIGUEL CHURCH TODAY

Today, the town is a quiet little village. The town square is not as well defined, and
the church has been remodeled since Abert painted it and Susan Magoffin visited it. It
is not as impressive on the outside as the original one visited by the early travelers.

Abert's Report of His Examination of New Mexico, 1846-47

PECOS RUINS

The ruins of Pecos was a major attraction for travelers along the Santa Fe Trail. Abert made his drawing in 1846, but the location can still be clearly identified. It appears that the lithographer added a little height to the hills and squared off the ruins.

Susan Magoffin noted on August 29, 1846, "I have visited this morning the ruins of an ancient pueblo, or village, now desolate and a home for wild beast and bird of the forest . . . . All around the church at diffeent distances are ruins . . ."

PECOS RUINS TODAY

The National Park Service has a walking path for self-guided tours for modern travelers and visitors.

National Archives

PECOS CATHEDRAL

This view shows the front of the ruins of the Catholic Church in 1846. Park historians question the scale of the ruins on the right when compared to the ruins of the church on the left.

On August 29, 1846, Susan Magoffin wrote, "The only part standing is the church. We got off our horses at the door and went in, and I was truly awed. I should think it was sixty by thirty . . . . From the church leads several doors, into private apartments of the priests, confession-rooms, penance chambers &c."

PECOS CATHEDRAL RUINS TODAY

When compared with the ruins of one hundred fifty years ago those of today have eroded greatly, but that feeling of awe can still be felt when one stands looking towards the altar. Today, the ruins have been stablized by the Park Service. Archeologists have also been working at the site.

Notes of a Military Reconnoissance, W.H. Emory

PECOS CATHEDRAL RUINS

This is another sketch of the church made in 1846. Note the kiva in the center of the drawing. Some park historians question the perspective and think it might have been reversed.

PECOS CATHEDRAL TODAY
Here is a similar view.

Ben Wittick # 15684, Museum of New Mexico

PECOS RUINS — OLD PHOTO

This is how the ruins looked in 1880 when photographed by Ben Wittick. By then local ranchers had already been using the ruins as a source of building materials, especially the wood. It was said that some ranchers had the finest looking fence posts in the country. As a result of this practice by them, the rate of deterioration increased.

PECOS RUINS TODAY

The photo below shows the results of continued deterioration, but also the restoration by the Park Service. Note the location of the kiva in both photos. This is thought to be the same one depicted in the drawing by Emory.

Today driving along I-25 makes the trip over Glorieta Pass and by Apache Canyon smooth and effortless. However, originally the route through Glorieta Pass and Apache Canyon was a very difficult one. Trader James Webb passed through the area in October, 1844, and wrote, "But a few miles from here we entered the big canyon, where the road winds and turns, crossing steep pitches and ravines, over rocks, and around boulders, making short and difficult turns, with double teams to make an Ascent. At other places the turns are so short that only two or three yoke of cattle can be allowed to pull the load, from danger of turning over into the ravine. One of these difficult passes we called the 'S,' which required all the skill of the best drivers to get around. And often wagons would be turned over with all the precautions we could use. Six or eight miles was considered good traveling.

"From the big canyon we cross a spur of the mountain, not very high but very steep and rough; so it was necessary to 'double' to get up. Thence through heavy pine timber and by a very rough and winding road to Arroyo Hondo, six miles from Santa Fe, where we camped for the night and made preparations to enter the long-sought end of our journey."

On August 30, 1846, Susan Magoffin wrote briefly of it, ". . . before noon I rode on horseback over all the bad places in the road, but this P.M. I have walked. It will not hurt me though, especially as much as jolting in the carriage over the hills and rough road we have passed, the being frightened half to death all the while."

Gregg saw the passage as less troublesome and wrote, "This mountain section of the road, even in its present unimproved condition, presents but few difficult passes, and might, with little labor, be put in good order." After the Mexican War the United States did improve the route for military reasons. Today Interstate Highway 85 parallels the general route of the Santa Fe Trail through Glorieta Pass, but the feel of the drive is very different.

Ben Wittick, Neg. No. 15782.
School of American Research Collections, Museum of New Mexico
PIGEON'S RANCH OVERVIEW — OLD PHOTO
This photo shows Pigeon's Ranch as it looked in June of 1880. The ranch was built right along the Santa Fe Trail in one of the narrow sections as the trail approached Glorieta Pass. The Santa Fe Trail can be seen as the road passing through the ranch. This ranch was the location of part of the famous Civil War Battle of Glorieta Pass which took place on March 28, 1862.

PIGEON'S RANCH TODAY

The photo below shows the same area today. Only a small portion of the ranch is still standing, and it can barely be seen through the trees that have grown up in the area.

Ben Wittick, Neg. No. 15783.
School of American Research Collections, Museum of New Mexico
PIGEON'S RANCH HOUSE
This closeup view is part of Pigeon's ranch that is shown in the larger photo. Wittick
had to have been standing on the roof of the building in the far lower left of the
other photo on page 166. Alexander Valle built the complex in the 1850s.

PIGEON'S RANCH BUILDING TODAY

Today only a low earthen pile outlines the location of most of Pigeon's ranch buildings. Only three small rooms from the main building shown in the photo above are still standing. They are from the far end of the building. It had been vandalized, but is presently being stabilized and restored. Note also that the tree at the edge of the rocky cliff above the ranch house in the old photo is still alive. The ranch is located on Highway 85A west of Pecos.

Here is Santa Fe (as drawn by Josiah Gregg) as it looked in the early 1840s before the United States defeated Mexico; in 1846 by Lt. Abert; and later in an old photo from the 1870s. All seem to be taken from the same general location looking down into the town. James Webb wrote in October, 1844, "The next morning we started at early dawn arrived on the loma (hill) overlooking the town about ten o'clock."

The Santa Fe Trail leading into the city is evident in all three. Note also the large parish church. Today a gothic structure has replaced it. Finding the exact spot where the artists were situated when they made the drawings is nearly impossible. Note also the lack of trees in the old sketches and photo. Today Santa Fe has grown tremendously, and homes are crowded together. Trees are everywhere and they now tower above what was almost a treeless plain.

Josiah Gregg, COMMERCE OF THE PRAIRIES
ARRIVAL AT SANTA FE

Abert—National Archives

SANTA FE IN 1846

Museum of New Mexico, # 10205

SANTA FE — OLD PHOTO

SANTA FE TODAY
Here is the view of Santa Fe as seen after leaving I-25 at the Old Pecos Road exit. There are so many trees and two story homes that the views in the old drawings and photo are impossible to duplicate.

Gregg arrived in Santa Fe ahead of his caravan in 1831. As he saw them enter he wrote ". . . the caravan at last hove in sight, and wagon after wagon was seen pouring down the last declivity at about a mile distance from the city. To judge from the clamerous rejoicings of the men, and the state of agreeable excitment which the muleteers seemed to be laboring under, the spectacle must have been as new to them as it had been to me. It was truly a scene for the artist's pencil to revel in. Even the animals seemed to participate in the humor of their riders, who grew more and more merry and obstreperous as they descended towards the city. I doubt, in short, whether the first sight of the walls of Jerusalem were beheld by the Crusaders with much more tumultuous and soul-enrapturing joy.

"The arrival produced a great deal of bustle and excitement among the natives. 'Los Americanos!' 'Los carros!' 'La entrada de la caravana!' were to be heard in every direction; and crowds of women and boys flocked around to see the new-comers; while the crowds of leperos hung about as usual to see what they could pilfer. The wagoners were by no means free from excitement on this occasion. Informed of the 'ordeal' they had to pass, they had spent the previous morning in 'rubbing up;' and now they were prepared, with clean faces, sleek combed hair, and their choisest Sunday suit, to meet the 'fair eyes' of the glistening black that were sure to stare at them as they passed. There was yet another preparation to be made in order to 'show off' to advantage. Each wagoner must tie a bran new 'cracker' to the lash of his whip; for, on driving through the streets and the plaza publica, every one strives to outvie his comrades in the dexterity with which he flourishes this favorite badge of his authority."

Museum of New Mexico, Neg. No. 11254
SANTA FE SQUARE — OLD PHOTO
This old photo shows the Ellsberg-Amberg wagon caravan in October 1861 in the
Santa Fe Plaza in front of the Governor's Place.

SANTA FE SQUARE TODAY
Below is a similar photo today. While vehicular traffic is banded from the plaza, it is
still a "hubbub" of local trade. In addition to all the shops around, the square is full
of sidewalk vendors trying to get your attention.

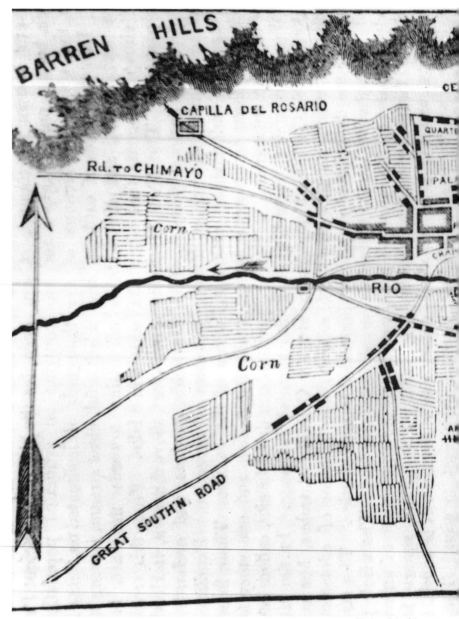

OLD MAP OF SANTA FE
This is a drawing showing the layout of Santa Fe in 1846 after it was taken over by the
United States.

BLOCK
HOUSE
FORT MARCY

N°.4.

N°3.   SP

Corn Fields

Paroquia

N°.2.

SANTA   FE

CAPILLA

1ST Reg M.M. Vol

No 1.   A B C U E F C H

rk

COL. DONIPHAN

Vol

ARMY ROUTE.

PRICE

Museum of New Mexico, # 45819

GOVERNOR'S PALACE — OLD PHOTO

The Governor's Palace was originally constructed around 1610 and is the oldest public building in the United States. Governor Manuel Armijo resided here before Kearny entered in 1846. Here, also were brought the early American explorers and traders such as Pike, McKnight, and Chouteau. This was also where the traders unloaded their goods for inspection. The last Governor resided here in 1912. The building has been renovated a number of times in its history as can be seen by comparing the photos.

GOVERNOR'S PALACE TODAY

Today, the Governor's Palace houses part of the Museum of New Mexico. This view is looking east down Palace Avenue.

Kansas State Historical Society

SAN MIGUEL CHAPEL — OLD PHOTO (rear view)

The mission, located at the southeast corner of Old Santa Fe Trail and De Vargas Street, was passed by all travelers as they entered Santa Fe. It seems to have been constructed no later than the early 1620s. It has been remodelled since then, but it has remained basically the same since trail days as is evident in today's photo. The photo from a side street shows the rear of the chapel. It now has a smooth coat covering the adobe bricks. Across the side street from the chapel is the "Oldest House" in Santa Fe. Notice all the trees in today's photo.

SAN MIGUEL CHAPEL TODAY

Library of Congress
SAN MIGUEL CHAPEL — OLD PHOTO
This is the frontal view of San Miguel taken during the Wheeler Expedition in 1873.
San Miguel is labelled as #1 on the old photo showing the approach to Santa Fe.

SAN MIGUEL CHAPEL TODAY

This photo shows the front looking at the other corner of the church. Another building and trees make it nearly impossible to take a photo from the same angle as the old photo. The white bell tower collapsed shortly after the old photo was taken. The new bell tower is quite different, but by looking closely, the line where the new tower and changes were made are evident.

Museum of New Mexico, # 11329

SAN FRANCISCO STREET — OLD PHOTO

These two scenes show the view east along San Francisco Street. The photo shows it as it appeared in 1868, while the drawing dates from the mid to late 1870s. Note the adobe Parish Church in the background in the top photo. The photo seems to have been taken from the roof of the buildling at the southwest corner of the Plaza. The scene shows wagons pulled by oxen lined up along the street. After the traders paid the duties, they sold their goods from the buildings around the plaza. The earliest caravan traders got the choice spots. In the later drawing the gothic structure, St. Francis Cathedral has replaced the adobe structure.

SAN FRANCISCO STREET — OLD DRAWING

Harper's Magazine

SAN FRANCISCO STREET TODAY

Today the streets are still full of people and activity. This similar photo was taken from ground level not the rooftop as the old photo was.

While the old Exchange Hotel was almost two blocks east, the hills in the background of the old drawing indicate the drawing was made west of the intersection of San Francisco and Don Gaspar. Standing at San Francisco and Don Gaspar one can almost hear the horses and stagecoaches coming around the corner.

National Archives—Abert

OLD PARISH CHURCH

This is the old Parish Church that the early traders saw. The drawing was made after the United States conquered New Mexico. Note the American Fort Marcy on the hill overlooking the city in the background. The old adobe church was replaced by the St. Francis Cathedral, a stone gothic structure, in the 1870s. It was constructed right over the site of the old church.

ST. FRANCIS CATHEDRAL TODAY

Harper's Magazine

ROAD TO TAOS

While Taos was not directly on the Santa Fe Trail for most traders, it did play a role
in its history and also that of New Mexico. The Sibley Survey went to Taos. The town
was also the home of many trappers, such as Kit Carson and Charles Bent. Here is a
sketch of the Road to Taos and also of the Indian Pueblo of Taos. The church in the
distance appears to be the one destroyed in the Taos Rebellion of 1847.

TAOS PUEBLO

Harper's Magazine

HIGHWAY TO TAOS
These are scenes similar to both the drawing of the Road to Taos and also to that of the Taos Pueblo. The ruins of the old church are not shown, but one of the two larger pueblos is shown.

TAOS PUEBLO TODAY

JEDEDIAH SMITH

Jedediah Smith was one of the West's most famous explorers and traders. He explored the West traveling to Ft. Vancouver in the Northwest and to San Gabriel in California. In 1831, he was killed by Indians while searching for water along the Cimarron River on the Santa Fe Trail.

MEMOIRS OF MY LIFE, John C. Fremont

KIT CARSON

Kit Carson has long been associated with the Santa Fe Trail. He was a trader, scout, and soldier. In 1826, at age sixteen, he ran away from home and joined a caravan to Santa Fe. He became a trapper and trader and his travels took him through much of the Rocky Mountains. He became a famous scout for the army serving both Fremont and Kearny in the 1840s. He served in the Civil War and later in the campaigns against the Indians in the Southwest and along the Santa Fe Trail. In 1867, he resigned his command from the army. He died in 1868.

CHARLES BENT

Brother of William, George, and Robert Bent, Charles was another of the famous traders associated with both the Indian and the Santa Fe trade. In 1833 William and Charles and Ceran St. Vrain built Bent's Fort on the Mountain Branch of the Santa Fe Trail. After Kearny invaded Mexico in 1846, he appointed Charles Bent as the first governor of the Territory of New Mexico. Bent was killed in the Taos Uprising on January 19, 1847.

WILLIAM BENT

William Bent was the brother of Charles, George, and Robert Bent. Bent's Fort was originally named Fort William when constructed in 1833. In 1849, William abandoned the old fort and destroyed part of it. By 1852, he was back in the trading business and built a new stone fort at Big Timbers. He also served as Indian agent for the government.

Museum of New Mexico, # 9896

JOSIAH GREGG

Josiah Gregg was the author of *Commerce Of The Prairies*. He first traveled to Santa Fe in 1831 under the advice of his physician. He hoped to regain his health. Gregg did more than that. He became a Santa Fe trader. His writing is the source of so much of the information known about the Southwest and Santa Fe. He retired from the Santa Fe trade in 1844.

Missouri Historical Society

SUSAN MAGOFFIN
This is the Susan Magoffin whose diary is referred to throughout much of this book.
She was only nineteen years old when she first went over the trail. She died in 1855
and is buried in Bellefontaine Cemetery in St. Louis.

SAMUEL MAGOFFIN

Samuel Magoffin, his young wife Susan, and his brothers James and William all had a role in the history of the Santa Fe Trail. The Magoffin family was long associated with the Santa Fe trade starting around 1830. In varying capacities they served both the Mexican and U.S. governments. By 1852, Susan and Samuel Magoffin were living near Kirkwood, Missouri. After Susan died, Samuel married her cousin, also named Susan Shelby. He died in 1888.

Denver Public Library, Western Collection
UNCLE DICK WOOTTON
Another scout and trader, he is most famous for building his toll road over the Raton Mountains and Pass. He blasted away rocks, straightned out sharp turns, built bridges and improved grades. No longer did it take five days to travel the twenty-seven miles. His toll road closed with the completion of the railroad over the mountain.

GENERAL STEPHEN WATTS KEARNY

General Stephen Watts Kearny joined the army during the War of 1812. Later he commanded a number of frontier army posts. He was appointed the leader of the United States forces that invaded Mexico and California during the Mexican War of 1846. His invasion route took the army over the Santa Fe Trail and along the Mountain Branch. In 1847, he was made governor of Veracruz and Mexico City. He died in 1848.

Majors House Foundation

ALEXANDER MAJORS

Alexander Majors became one of the major figures in the freighting business that developed in the west. His companies carried much of the goods and materials for the army. In 1859, the freighting company of Russell, Majors, and Waddell had 4,796 wagons, 46,720 oxen, 4,380 mules, and employed 4,680 men. Majors issued each man a BIBLE and required his employees to take the following oath:

"While I am in the employ of A. Majors, I agree not to use profane language, not to get drunk, not to gamble, not to treat animals cruelly, and not to do anything else that is incompatible with the conduct of a gentlemen. And I agree, if I violate any of the above conditions, to accept my discharge without pay for my services."

Later, he was also one of the founders of the famous, but short-lived, Pony Express.

Harper's Magazine

CAUGHT IN THE SNOW

One of the problems faced by caravans and travelers over the prairies was getting caught in a snow storm. For the traders trying to extend the traveling season, it could prove deadly for both animal and human.

The opening of the National Frontier Trails Center was almost delayed by a severe snow storm which dumped nearly a foot of snow the afternoon and evening it opened. A simulated prairie camp had been set up for the opening. However, by 10:00 P.M. the cold and snow were so bad that the last hearty person gave up the campsite for the warmth of a truck camper. By 8:00 A.M. the sun was up and the abandoned camp looked like this.

SNOWBOUND CAMP TODAY

ADVERTISEMENT — WAGON

This is an advertisement for the Murphy Wagons that became famous along the Santa Fe Trail.

ADVERTISEMENT — STORE

This is a copy of an ad for the Conn Store in Council Grove.

SANTA FE FREIGHT WAGON

Here are two typical wagons associated with the trails west. The one above is the freight wagon, and the one below is the emigrant wagon. Note the differences in the number of wagon bows, the length of the wagon beds, and height of the wagon boxes.

EMIGRANT WAGON

CONESTOGA WAGON
This Conestoga Wagon had been on display at Bent's Fort. It is now housed at Fort Larned. Note the curved wagon bed and raked ends.

SANTA FE WAGON CAMP
This scene, taken in 1880, shows the teamsters and freight wagons in camp in Santa Fe near the old state house.

Ben Wittick, Museum of New Mexico, # 15817

GRAVE TODAY

Samuel Hunt was a private in the U.S. Army who explored west along the Platte River, south along the Rockies, and back east along the Santa Fe Trail. He was the only casualty on the 1835 expedition. His grave is one of the earliest known marked graves along the Santa Fe Trail.

BENT'S FORT — ABERT'S FLOOR PLAN

Lt. J.W. Abert made this sketch of the floor plan of Bent's Fort when he visited it. Like almost all structures in this area at that time, the fort was constructed of adobe bricks. Later when the fort was being reconstructed by the National Parks Service, the sketch was very useful.

Western America in 1846-47: The Original Travel Diary of Lieutenant J.W. Abert,
Ed. John Galvin, John Howell Books

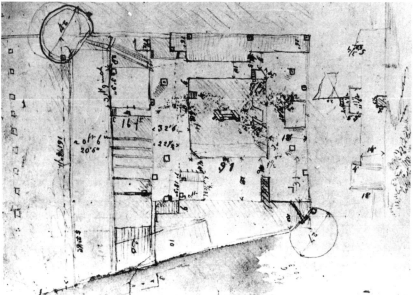

Part IV
Museums and Displays

Museums & Displays

FOR THE MODERN traveler there are a number of museums, displays, and landmarks along the highways that follow or parallel the old Santa Fe Trail. Nineteen areas and sites have been identified. Some of these areas include numerous historic sites while others only one. In addition, there are other smaller museums and sites in many of the small towns and along the highways. They vary in size and scope from mere signs noting wagon ruts to fine town museums. Of the sites located below, some would require three or more days to tour in order to enjoy the whole experience, while others can be visited in a few hours or less.

Jefferson National Expansion Memorial, St. Louis, Missouri

This is one of the finest museums covering the whole period of westward expansion. It is built on the site of the original St. Louis settlement. It is located under the "Gateway Arch" which symbolizes the role that St. Louis played as the "Gateway to the West." Within the museum are displays, exhibits, and interpretive programs covering all the major themes and events associated with the exploration and settlement of the West. Also nearby are other sites and buildings such as the Old Courthouse, Old Cathedral, the Sappling House, and Laclede's Landing Historic District.

The archway is located on the west bank of the Mississippi River near the intersection of I-70 and I-55.

Another point of interest is the Bellefontaine Cemetery between Broadway and West Florissant off I-70, exit 245. Samuel and Susan Magoffin, James Magoffin, General Stephan Kearny, and Senator Thomas Hart Benton, all figures associated with the Santa Fe Trail, are buried there.

Arrow Rock State Historic Site, Missouri

This quaint historic town was platted in 1829 by Meredith M. Marmaduke, one of the men associated with the Santa Fe trade. It is situated on a bluff above the major Indian rendezvous and crossing area of the Missouri River. Before the town was platted the site was also the rendezvous area for traders from both Franklin and Boonville before they started on to Santa Fe. Here is found the famous Santa Fe Spring whose setting is as it was in trail days. Many a teamster filled his wagon's water barrels from this spring before heading out. The town itself has many buildings associated with the mid trail period. In the 1834 Huston Tavern one can dine in the same place that Kit Carson, Senator Benton, and other famous individuals associated with the Trail's history did. There are a number of restored buildings that are open to the public. Antique shops, bed and breakfast establishments, and a theater enhance the town's appeal. Arrow Rock State Park is located here and camping facilities are available. Originally the town of Arrow Rock was called New Philadelphia, but its name was soon changed back to reflect its early Indian heritage. A new visitor center was scheduled to open in 1991.

Arrow Rock is located about fourteen miles east of Marshall on Missouri Highway 41 or thirteen miles north off I-70 on exit 98.

Fort Osage National Historic Landmark, Missouri

Fort Osage was originally built in 1808. It was the first Army post west of the Mississippi and served as Milepost Zero during the Sibley survey of the Santa Fe Trail in 1825. The fort and buildings have been carefully reconstructed on their original sites according to their original plans. The museum and displays cover the period associated with the early fur trade and Santa Fe Trail.

It is located about fourteen miles northeast of Independence in Sibley, three and one-half miles north of US 24 on County Road 20-E.

Fort Osage is a registered National Historic Landmark and is under the jurisdiction of the Jackson County Parks and Recreation.

Independence, Westport, Kansas City Area

This area became the major jumping-off site for the Santa Fe Trail from the late 1820s until the early 1840s. For a brief period in the mid to late 1840s it also served as the major outfitting place for travelers on the Oregon and California Trails.

Within the Independence area are numerous sites associated with the trails period. Independence Square is often considered the starting point of the three great western trails. Nearby are the Brady Cabin and Independence Spring, the old log courthouse, the Waggoner home, the newly opened National Frontier Trails Center, the Fitzhugh-Watts Mill site, the Alexander Majors house, old Westport, Westport Landing, the Rice Farm, Cave Spring, Minor Park, and the Shawnee Methodist Mission. These are but a few of the historic sites associated with the trails located in this area. To visit and enjoy all of these sites a visitor would take a few days.

Fort Leavenworth, Kansas

This fort was established by the U.S. Army to protect trade on the Santa Fe Trail. It is the oldest continuously operated military facility west of the Mississippi. It was established in 1827 and is still an active military post and the home of the U.S. Army Command and General Staff College. This was the base from which the earliest military escorts left in 1829 to protect the traders, and where Colonel Kearny assembled his army that invaded

Mexico in 1846. It also became another of the jumping-off sites for emigrants going to Oregon and California. The oldest buildling, the Rookery, dates from 1832, and the trail ruts leading up the bluff from the landing area are still visible. There is a fine museum which covers the complete military period of Fort Leavenworth.

It is located off highway US 73, just north of present-day Leavenworth, Kansas.

Council Grove, Kansas

This was a major camping area and organizational point for the caravans heading down the Santa Fe Trail. It is located at the crossing of the Neosho River and was the last major source of hard wood along the trail. As one approaches and leaves the Council Grove area, impressive views of the rolling prairies can be seen. There are numerous sites associated with the trail here: the great Council Oak where the Council Grove Treaty of 1825 was signed; the Post Office Oak; the Conn Store; the Hays Tavern; the Kaw Mission; and the Last Chance Store. Walking and driving guides are available. In addition to these, there are numerous other historical sites in the area.

It is located on highway US 56.

Pawnee Rock

This is one of the major landmarks along the Santa Fe Trail. Today it is less impressive than it was to the early traders and travelers who then saw it rising as a small wart on the treeless prairie. It served as an autograph rock for the traders and travelers. Unfortunately, today the names of the early traders are all gone. Also, it seems that Pawnee Rock was also used by early settlers as a quarry. However, standing on the viewing tower one can still experience the same feeling of awe at the panoramic view that the early emigrants did when standing on top.

It is located about fourteen miles southwest of Great Bend on US Highway 56 at Pawnee Rock.

Santa Fe Trail Center Museum, Larned, Kansas

This is the location of the Santa Fe Trail Center. The museum's exhibits depict the life on the Santa Fe Trail and frontier of the 1800s.

It is located a few miles west of Larned on State Route 156.

Fort Larned National Historic Site, Kansas

This fort became the major post on the eastern section of the Santa Fe Trail after it was first established in 1859. In 1860, the post was moved to its present location. Today it has been restored to its splendor of its trail days and has one of the best museums and living history displays along the trail. With the reconstruction of the blockhouse its restoration is almost complete. Nearby in a detached site, are some of the best preserved trail ruts in the area. In addition, there is a prairie dog town, evidence of buffalo wallows, and a place where one can enjoy the feelings and scents of the prairie.

Fort Larned is located six miles west of Larned on Kansas Highway 156.

State Buffalo Preserve, Garden City, Kansas

While this preserve is not directly on the trail itself, it is situated across the Arkansas from the trail. One of the major sights and thrills experienced by the Santa Fe travelers was seeing the great buffalo herds on the prairie. Today one can still come close to experiencing similar thrills by visiting the Buffalo Preserve and by taking a guided drive through the 3,800 acre preserve.

This is one stop that should not be missed by anyone, young or old. Not only does one experience the prairie as it must have been to the earlier travelers, but one sees the buffalo close up roaming freely in waist high prairie grasses.

The State Buffalo Preserve is located south of Garden City on US 83 just south of the Arkansas River.

Bent's Old Fort National Historic Site, Colorado

This site is on the Mountain Branch of the Santa Fe Trail. Bent's Old Fort has been painstakingly reconstructed on the original site after many years of intensive study and archaeological work. As the visitor walks up to the fort and then inside, it is as if one enters a time capsule back to Santa Fe Trail days. Inside, the fort has been furnished to appear as it did to the earlier traders and travelers. The living displays add a fine touch which brings the visitor back in time. This is where Susan Magoffin stopped to recuperate and where Colonel Kearny prepared for the U.S. invasion of Mexico in 1846. Special events are scheduled for various times of the year, so try to plan your visit in conjunction with them.

The fort is located about eight miles east of La Junta on Colorado Highway 194.

Trinidad, Colorado, and Raton Mountains

Trinidad grew up on the Santa Fe Trail within sight of Fisher's Peak and the Raton Mountains on the Mountain Branch of the Santa Fe Trail. Located in the city is the Baca/Bloom Pioneer Museum complex. The Baca House is a two story adobe structure that was built in 1870 by merchant John Hough. The Bloom House was built in 1882. Both homes have been furnished as they might have appeared at the time of their construction and at the end of the Santa Fe Trail period. The Museum has displays encompassing the early history of the area. Its collection includes Kit Carson's famous plains jacket. The complex is under the care of the Colorado Historical Society.

Just south of Trinidad the Santa Fe Trail started up to cross the Raton Mountains. This portion of the trail was one of the slowest and most dangerous, taking a week or more to make. Only with the building of Uncle Dick Wootton's Toll Road, and, later, the railroad, did the crossing become safer and faster. However, for the modern traveler the pull up the mountain will be measured in minutes. The Santa Fe Railroad closely follows the route of the trail until it goes through the tunnel under Raton Mountain. Interstate 25 generally follows the route of the trail. For most of the trip from Trinidad to Raton the trail is to the west of the Interstate. At the pass, the trail is about one half mile to the west. By looking back down the mountainside the traveler can see the difficult climb the traders had.

Cimarron, New Mexico
This is the location of the Lucien Maxwell Ranch. It was part of an original land grant which comprised about 1,700,000 acres. Cimarron and Rayado, further to the south, became the center of Maxwell's operation. Still standing in Cimarron is the old mill, now operating as a museum. Also in Cimarron is the St. James Hotel which was constructed during the last years of the Santa Fe Trail. Most of its history is associated with the post Santa Fe Trail era. It has been refurbished and has all the atmosphere of the early wild west. It is a very interesting place in which to stay or to dine. There are a number of other historic sites in Cimarron that date from the trail days.

Cimarron is located on US Highway 64 and historic

Cimarron is south off 64 on State Route 21 across the Cimarron River.

Wagon Bed Spring, National Historic Landmark, Ulysses, Kansas

This small spring site by the dry bed of the Cimarron was the goal of the Santa Fe traders as they crossed the Jornada after two or three days of hot, dusty, waterless travel. This was the site Jedediah Smith was looking for when he was attacked and killed by Comanches in May of 1831.

It is located about ten miles south of Ulysses off Highway 25 on an improved dirt road near where the roadway crosses the Cimarron.

Rabbit Ears and Round Mound, Clayton, New Mexico

These landmarks are two of the most famous on the Santa Fe Trail. Traders could first see Rabbit Ears on the horizon by looking southwest east of McNees Crossing near the present Oklahoma-New Mexico border. It is said to have received its name not from its shape, but from a Cheyenne Chief Rabbit Ears who was killed here by the Spanish.

From Turkey Creek camp, north of Rabbit Ears, Round Mound was the next landmark for the traders as they continued southwest along the trail. This ancient volcanic dome sits out on the flat prairie for all to see. The trail passed the north side of it. Many a trader climbed it to view the surrounding area. (See photo section.) Even today the view is spectacular, but the climb is difficult and dangerous. The distance and height is deceiving on the prairie and rattlesnakes still inhabit the mountain.

Both landmarks can be seen west of Clayton along US Highway 64 and 87. Rabbit Ears is about six miles north off Highway 370, and the Round Mound marker is about twenty-two miles west on US Highway 64 and 87.

Wagon Mound, New Mexico

This was the last major landmark along the Santa Fe Trail. It was located on the Cimarron Cutoff. It was first visible to travelers from near Point of Rocks east of the Rock Crossing of the Canadian River. It was then almost in constant sight for two days as they approached it to the south. While the Mountain Branch did not pass by it, Wagon Mound could first be seen on the horizon far to the south from near Cimarron. In the trail's early days Wagon Mound was also likened to a shoe. However, its silhouette reminded other traders of a wagon and team headed west, and that seems to be how it received its name. This was the site of the mail coach massacre in May, 1850. At the base is an old cemetery and the grave of Charles Fraker, a freighter on the Santa Fe Trail. Also located near here is the Santa Clara Spring and campground of freighting days.

The best view of Wagon Mound is from Interstate 25 as one approaches it from the north or along the parallel old highway. Wagon Mound is located just east off Interstate 25 on Highway 120.

Between Wagon Mound and Watrous are some of the finest examples of wagon ruts along the Santa Fe Trail today. The best are paralleling the north side of Interstate 25 as it approaches Watrous from about eight miles out.

Fort Union National Monument, New Mexico

Fort Union is located near where the Mountain Branch and the Cimarron Cutoff joined. It became the guardian of the Santa Fe Trail after it was first built in 1851. Not only did it serve as a fort, but also as the supply depot for all the forts in the Southwest. Its ruins, visitor center, museum, displays, and living history programs makes it one of the highlights on the Santa Fe Trail today.

It is located eight miles north of Watrous on State Highway 477.

For the east bound caravans the Las Vegas-Watrous area near the Mora played a role similar to that of Council Grove on the far eastern section of the trail. The campgrounds in the area served as a rendezvous for traders heading east. Here larger caravans were formed before heading into the dangerous Indian territory on the plains. The Watrous house, Sapello Stage Station, and Fort Union Corral are located near Watrous.

Pecos National Monument and Glorieta Pass, New Mexico

While this site did not play a direct role in the development of Santa Fe Trail, it was one of the sites most frequently mentioned by travelers. It was founded in the fifteenth century, and by the early 1620s, the Franciscans had founded a mission at Pecos. At one time the pueblo was home to two thousand Indians. The mission was finally abandoned in 1782 and was in ruins when the Santa Fe traders came through. But, it was those ruins which impressed the early travelers. Today, the ruins are greatly deteriorated compared to those seen by the early traders, but the National Park Service has stabilized them. Visitors can walk around and see ruins from Pecos' different historic periods. There is a fine visitor center and museum.

Old Pecos is located off Interstate 25, four miles north on Highway 63.

West of Pecos the Santa Fe Trail entered Glorieta Pass and then Apache Canyon. This was the site of the Civil War Battle of Glorieta Pass, March 26–28, 1862.

The Union Army's base camp was located east of Old Pecos at Koziowski's ranch, now the Forked Lightning Ranch. One of the major battles was at the Pigeon Ranch, one mile south of the interchange of I-25 and SR 50 toward Pecos. Only a portion of the Pigeon Ranch now stands. Johnson's Ranch site, another location of the Civil War battle, was off the I-25 294 exit.

Santa Fe, New Mexico

This was the end of the Santa Fe Trail for many of the merchants and traders. Some, however, continued south to Chihuahua deep in Mexico.

Santa Fe today retains much of its charm and is still a trading town for tourists. Within Santa Fe is the famous Plaza with its Palace of the Governors. The palace is now part of the Museum of New Mexico. Nearby is the St. Francis Cathedral, the site of Fort Marcy, San Miguel Chapel rebuilt in 1710 and remodelled again in the mid–1870s, the "Oldest House," and the grave of Charles Bent. Visitors should plan on spending a few days in the Santa Fe region to see and enjoy all the historic sites and shops. It still has a flavor all its own. And, for those who desire culture of another sort, there is the Santa Fe Opera Company.

Taos, New Mexico

While Santa Fe was the end of the trail, Taos was the official end of the trail surveyed by Sibley in 1825. Taos is an old Indian Pueblo and old Spanish town. This is where Charles Bent, Governor of New Mexico, lived and was killed by Indians during the Taos Revolt in 1847. A portion of his house is open. Taos was also the home of Kit Carson and his house is now a fine museum. Carson is also buried in Taos. A few miles north is the famous Taos Pueblo which is worth a visit.

Taos is located about seventy-five miles north of Santa Fe on US 64.

Part V
Background

Recommended Reading

A WIDE VARIETY OF books are available on the Santa Fe Trail. Some of these are considered classics about trail travel and the history of the Southwest. In recent years there has been a renewed interest in the Santa Fe Trail, and that is reflected in the books now available.

Two authors have written books which take the modern traveler along the Santa Fe Trail from Franklin, Missouri to Santa Fe, New Mexico. The first by Marc Simmons is his *Following The Santa Fe Trail, A Guide For Modern Travelers* published in 1984 and just recently updated. Simmons explains some of the basic information travelers should know about present trail travel, the history of its marking, and the history of the trail. It takes the traveler from one site to another. Included is a weath of material about all the specific sites found at each location. It provides some additional information that is not found in Brown's book mentioned later. Simmons' work is interspersed with small general maps, but they highlight only the major sites and areas along the main highways.

Two of the most recent books were both written by Gregory Franzwa. The two books actually supplement each other. *Maps Of The Santa Fe Trail* and *The Santa Fe Trail Revisited* were both published in 1989.

Maps Of The Santa Fe Trail is for the traveler who can read and follow maps and can visualize the trip. The emphasis is on the main Santa Fe Trail from Franklin, Missouri to Santa Fe, but the book also includes many of the very important cutoffs and alternate routes that developed over the years. The trail shows up as a thin red line on the maps. Franzwa's work shows the whole continuous route using ninety-nine pages of maps. Most of the maps are drawn having a scale of one-half inch to a mile and include not only the main highways and roads, but also the farm roads. For those readers familiar with his Oregon Trail books, you will know how useful this is. The location of large segments of visible trail ruts are also located on the maps as are the related historic sites. Therefore, they are much easier for the present day traveler to find and see.

The Santa Fe Trail Revisited takes the reader turn by turn and mile by mile along the modern highways and farm roads that most closely follow the twists and turns of the old Santa Fe Trail. Along with this milepost approach are comments from various traders and emigrants who took the route described or stopped to rest where the modern traveler can. Places where the modern traveler might not be able to venture in a passenger car are noted. The important historic sites along the way are also mentioned and the significance of each site is explained.

Another related book is *The Santa Fe Trail; The National Park Service 1963 Historic Sites Survey* by William E. Brown published in 1988. It identifies the location of fifty-three general sites of historic significance. Many of these sites are actually composed of different historic points of interest, but they have been grouped together as one because of their proximity to each other. These same sites are also located in both of Franzwa's and Simmons' books. The sites include things such as buildings, ruins, major forts, crossings, landmarks, and even prominent camping grounds, and often include comments about each place by early travelers.

These four books make locating and traveling along the Santa Fe Trail today easy and enjoyable.

Two other items deserve to be mentioned. One is Stanley Kimball's *Historic Sites And Markers Along The Mormon And Other Great Western Trails*, which includes the Santa Fe Trail as the route used by the Mormon Battalion in 1846 as it marched to Santa Fe and then to

California. Another trail book is a small, inexpensive pamphlet. Gene and Mary Martin's *Trail Dust* gives the reader a quick overview of the trail's history.

For a historic view of the development of the Santa Fe Trail there are a few books.

Henry Inman was a Colonel in the U.S. Army in the 1800s. His book, *The Old Santa Fe Trail, The Story Of A Great Highway*, was one of the first to be solely concerned with the historic development of the trail. It was published in 1897. It is full of interesting stories of the people and adventures based on his own experiences or those related to him about events and the times of the trail. However, more recent investigations have opened questions about some of his material. Also, because of its age it is even hard to find in some libraries. Keeping these factors in mind, it is still a good beginning.

Another is Robert Duffus' *The Santa Fe Trail*. It also covers the development of the trail from its beginning to its end with the coming of the railroad. While it was first published in 1930, it is still available. And even today, it is considered an excellent beginning for a more detailed and accurate study of the trail's history.

One of the most recent and scholarly books covering the development of the trail is Seymour Connor's and James Skaggs', *Broadcloth And Britches, The Santa Fe Trade*, published in 1977.

In addition to the scholarly appraoch to the study of the Santa Fe Trail there are a number of narratives and diaries of travelers along the trail.

Josiah Gregg's *Commerce Of The Prairie* is considered to be the classic account of trade from 1831–1844. It was originally published in 1846 in two volumes. It is more than a history of the trail. It is full of the personal adventures of a man who crossed the trail eight times. Not only are there descriptions about the trail, its geography, its dangers, the wagons, the daily routines and sites, there is additional wealth of information about the culture of the Southwest. Described are the animals—domestic and wild, the government, the local industries, daily life, and culture of both the Indians and Mexicans. This is the book to read. Brown calls it, "The Bible for the student of the trail."

The second most important book to read is Susan Magoffin's diary, edited by Stella Drumm, *Down The Santa Fe Trail And Into Mexico*. This is a woman's story of her honeymoon trip down to Santa Fe and Chihuahua. It provides many insights about the trail and what it was in 1846-7 during the Mexican War. If you obtain only one diary, this is the one. It is also the book to have on your car seat to read as you travel along the trail.

Another fine book available is *Land Of Enchantment, Memoirs Of Marian Russell Along The Santa Fe Trail*, edited by Garnet Brayer. Her stories of her travels and life in the Southwest helps one understand both the hard times and the romance of the trail.

There are many other fine books about the trail which deserve to be mentioned. Marc Simmons has another book, *On The Santa Fe Trail*, which is comprised of letters and narratives by travelers along the trail. *Wah-To-Yah & The Taos Trail* by Lewis H. Garrard tells of a teenage boy's adventures on the trail and in the southwest; *Adventures In The Santa Fe Trade, 1844-47*, by James Josiah Webb, continues the story of the traders after Josiah Gregg wrote; and *Matt Field On The Santa Fe Trail*, edited by John E. Sunder, tells of some of the reporter's episodes along the trail.

For reviewing the material available as of 1971 there is Jack D. Rittenhouse's *The Santa Fe Trail, A Historical Bibliography*. This is a brief, but excellent review of the works known at that time. Since then, there have been additional works found and written.

Additionally, the journals of the various state and local

historical societies are fine sources for journals and materials and should not be overlooked. The publication of the Santa Fe Trail Association, *Wagon Tracks*, published quarterly, is another excellent source of material. It includes information about the present condition of the trail, efforts aimed at its preservation, stories of past travelers, chapter notes, and information about museums and sites. There are also many other books which focus on particular topics. For trivia lovers, there is Leo and Bonita Oliva's *Santa Fe Trail Trivia*. Others, *Bent's Fort* by David Lavender; *Soldiers On The Santa Fe Trail* by Leo Oliva; *Seventy Years On The Frontier* by Alexander Majors; *Uncle Dick Wootton* by Howard Louis Conrad; *Kit Carson's Autobiography* edited by Milo Milton Quaife; *Broken Hand: Life of Thomas Fitzpatrick, Mountain Man Guide And Indian Agent* by Leroy Hafen, and *Jedediah Smith And The Opening Of The West* by Dale Morgan are but a few of the books dealing with individuals and specific aspects of the trail's history. If you like stories and tales about Kansas and the Santa Fe Trail there is Dary's *True Tales Of Old-Time Kansas*. One last area which must be mentioned is the bibliographies of all the books mentioned. They are full of outstanding source materials which you may find of interest.

Happy Reading! Happy Traveling!

Bibliography

BOOKS, BOOKLETS, AND ARTICLES

Barry, Louise, *The Beginning Of The West: Annals Of The Kansas Gateway To The American West*, 1540–1854. Topeka: Kansas State Historical Society, 1972.

Bott, Emily Ann O'Neil, "Joseph Murphy's Contribution To The Development Of The West", Missouri Historical Review. Vol. 47, No. 1 (Oct. 1952), pp. 18–28.

Brown, William E., *The Santa Fe Trail, National Park Service 1963 Historic Sites Survey*. St. Louis: Patrice Press, 1988.

Connor, Seymour & Jummy Skaggs, *Broadcloth And Britches: The Santa Fe Trade*. College Station: Texas A&M University Press, 1977.

Conrad, Howard Louis, *Uncle Dick Wootton, The Pioneer Frontiersman Of The Rocky Mountains*. Lincoln: University of Nebraska Press, 1980.

Dary, David, *True Tales Of Old-Time Kansas*. Lawrence: University of Kansas Press, 1987.

DeVoto, Bernard, *The Year Of Decision*. Boston: Little, Brown and Company, 1943.

Driggs, Howard Roscoe, *Westward America*. New York: Somerset Books, Inc. 1942.

Duffus, Robert L., *The Santa Fe Trail*. New York: Longmans, Green & Co., 1931.

Eggenhofer, Nick, *Wagons, Mules And Men: How The Frontier Moved West*. New York: Hastings House Publishers, 1961.

Estergreen, M. Morgan, *Kit Carson; A Portrait In Courage*. Norman: University of Oklahoma Press, 1962.

Franzwa, Gregory, *Maps Of The Oregon Trail*. Gerald: Patrice Press, 1982.

Franzwa, Gregory, *Maps Of The Santa Fe Trail*. St. Louis: Patrice Press, 1989.

Franzwa, Gregory, *The Santa Fe Trail Revisited*. St. Louis: Patrice Press, 1989.

Franzwa, Gregory, *Images Of The Santa Fe Trail*. St. Louis: Patrice Press, 1988.

Gardner, Mark L. ed., *The Mexican Road, Trade, Travel, and Confrontation on the Santa Fe Trail*. Manhattan, Kansas: The Sunflower Press, 1989.

Gilbert, William, and others, *The Trail Blazers*. New York: Time/Life Books, 1973.

Hafen, LeRoy R., *Broken Hand: The Life Story Of Thomas Fitzpatrick, Chief Of The Mountain Men*. Denver: The Old West Publishing Co., 1931.

Haines, Aubrey, *Historic Sites Along The Oregon Trail.* St. Louis: Patrice Press, 1981.

Hamilton, Jean T., *Arrow Rock, Where Wheels Started West.* Friends of Arrow Rock, 1971.

Hill, William E., *The California Trail, Yesterday And Today,* Boulder: Pruett Publishing Co., 1986.

Hill, William E., *The Oregon Trail, Yesterday And Today.* Caldwell, Idaho: The Caxton Printers, Ltd., 1987.

Horn, Houston, *The Pioneers.* New York: Time/Life Books, 1974.

Inman, Col. Henry, *The Old Santa Fe Trail, The Story Of A Great Highway.* Topeka: Crane & Co., 1916.

Kimball, Stanley B., *Historic Sites And Markers Along The Mormon And Other Great Western Trails.* Urbana: University of Illinois Press, 1988.

Lavender, David, *Bent's Fort.* New York: Doubleday & Co., 1954.

Laxalt, Robert, and others, *Trails West.* Washington, D.C.: National Geographic Society, 1979.

Martin, Gene and Mary, *Trail Dust: A Quick Picture History Of The Santa Fe Trail.* Martin Associates, 1972.

Moody, Ralph, *The Old Trails West.* New York: T.Y. Crowell Co., 1963.

Morgan, Dale L., *Jedediah Smith And The Opening Of The West.* Indianapolis: The Bobbs-Merrill Co., Inc., 1953.

Oliva, Leo, *Fort Larned.* Topeka: Kansas State Historical Society, 1985.

Oliva, Leo, *Soldiers On The Santa Fe Trail.* Norman: University of Oklahoma Press, 1967.

Oliva, Leo E. & Bonita M., *Santa Fe Trail Trivia.* Western Books, 1989.

Quaife, Milo Milton, *Kit Carson's Autobiography.* Lincoln: University of Nebraska Press, 1966.

Richardson, Albert D., *Beyond The Mississippi.* Hartford: American Publishing Company, 1869.

Rittenhouse, Jack D., *The Santa Fe Trail, A Historical Bibliography.* Albuquerque, 1968.

Rittenhouse, Jack D., *Trail Of Commerce And Conquest: A Brief History of the Road to Santa Fe.* Woodston: Santa Fe Trail Council, 1987.

Simmons, Marc, *Following The Santa Fe Trail: A Guide For Modern Travelers.* Santa Fe: Ancient City Press, 1984.

Simmons, Marc, "Part I: The Old Trail To Santa Fe," *Overland Journal,* Vol. 4, No. 2 (Spring 1986), pp. 4–15.

Simmons, Marc, "Part II: The Old Santa Fe Trail," *Overland Journal,* Vol. 4, No. 3 (Summer 1986), pp. 61–9.

Simmons, Marc, "Part III: The Old Santa Fe Trail," *Overland Journal,* Vol. 4, No. 4 (Fall 1986), pp. 65–77.

Simmons, Marc, *Along The Santa Fe Trail*. Photos by Joan Myers. Albuquerque: University of New Mexico Press, 1986.

Taylor, Morris, *First Mail West, Stage Coach Lines On The Santa Fe Trail*. Albuquerque: University of New Mexico Press, 1971.

Unruh, John, *The Plains Across, The Overland Emigrants And The Trans-Mississippi West, 1840-60*. Chicago: University of Illinois Press, 1979.

Utley, Robert M., *Fort Union National Monument*. National Park Service, 1962.

Walker, Henry Pickering, *The Wagon Masters: High Plains Freighting From The Earliest Days Of The Santa Fe Trail To 1880*. Norman: University of Oklahoma, 1966.

Wheat, Carl I., *Mapping The Trans-Mississippi West, 1540-1861*, 5 Vols. San Francisco: Institute of Historical Cartography, 1957-63.

Wheeler, George M., *Wheeler's Photographic Survey Of The American West, 1871-73: With 50 Landscape Photographs By Timothy O'Sullivan And William Bell*. New York: Dover Publications, 1983.

Wilcox, Pearl, *Jackson County Pioneers*. Pearl Wilcox.

DIARIES, JOURNALS, AND GUIDEBOOKS

Abert, Lt. J.W., *Through The Country Of The Comanche Indians In The Fall Of The Year 1845, The Journal Of A U.S. Army Expedition Led By Lieutenant J.W. Abert Of The Topographical Engineers*, Ed. John Galvin. John Howell Books, 1970.

Abert, Lt. J.W., *Western America In 1846-7, The Original Travel Diary Of Lieutenant J.W. Abert*, Ed. John Galvin. John Howell Books, 1954.

Brewerton, George Douglas, "A Ride with Kit Carson," *Harper's New Monthly Magazine*, Vol. 7, No. 39 (August, 1853), pp. 447-66.

Brewerton, George Douglas, "Incidents of Travel in New Mexico," *Harper's New Monthly Magazine*, Vol. 8, No. 47 (April, 1854), pp. 577-96.

Brewerton, George Douglas, "In the Buffalo Country," *Harper's New Monthly Magazine*, Vol. 25, No. 148 (September, 1862), pp. 447-66.

Bryant, Edwin, *What I Saw In California*. New York: D. Appleton and Co., 1849.

Davis, Theodore R., "Winter on the Plains," *Harper's New Monthly Magazine*, Vol. 39 (June, 1869), pp. 22-34.

Emory, William H., *Notes Of A Military Reconnoisance, From Fort Leavenworth, In Missouri, To San Diego, In California, Including Part Of The Arkansas, Del Norte, And Gila Rivers*. U.S. 30th Congress, 1st Session, H.R. Exec. Doc. 41. Washington, 1848.

Farnham, Thomas Jefferson, *Travels In The Great Western Prairies, The Anahuac And Rocky Mountains, And In The Oregon Territory*. New York: Greeley & McElrath, 1843 (reprint Rodern R. McCallum, 1977).

Fremont, John Charles, *The Expeditions Of J.C. Fremont, Vol. I, II, & Maps*, ed. Donald Jackson and Mary Lee Spence. Urbana: University of Illinois Press, 1970.

Fremont, John Charles, *Memoirs Of My Life*. New York: Belford, Clarks & Co., 1887.

Drumm, Stella M., ed. *Down The Santa Fe Trail And Into New Mexico: The Dairy Of Susan Shelby Magoffin, 1846-47*. Lincoln: University of Nebraska Press, 1982.

Garrard, Lewis H., *Wah-To-Yah And The Taos Trail*. Palo Alto, California: American West Publishing Co., 1968.

Gregg, Josiah, *Commerce Of The Prairies, Vol. I & II*. New York: Henry G. Langley, 1844 (Reprint Ann Arbor: University of Michigan. Microfilm, Inc. 1966).

Gregg, Kate L., ed. *The Road To Santa Fe*. (Journal of George C. Sibley-1825, 1826, & 1827; Diary of Joseph Davis-1825; Diary of Benjamin H. Reeves-1825) Albuquerque: University of New Mexico Press, 1952.

Heap, Gwinn Harris, *Central Route To The Pacific, From The Valley Of The Mississippi To California: Journal Of The Expedition Of E.F. Beale, Superintendent Of Indian Affairs In California, And Gwinn Harris Heap, From Missouri To California*. Ed. LeRoy R. & Ann W. Hafen. Glendale: Arthur H. Clark, Co., 1957.

Kendall, George W., *Narrative Of An Expedition Across The Great Southwest Prairies, From Texas To Santa Fe, Vol. I & II*. London: David Bogue, 1845 (Reprint Ann Arbor: University of Michigan. Microfilm, Inc. 1966).

Majors, Alexander, *Seventy Years On The Frontier: Alexander Major's Memors Of A Lifetime On The Border*. Ed. Prentis Ingraham. New York: Rand, McNally & Co., 1893.

Marcy, Randolph B., *The Prairie Traveler, A Handbook For Overland Expeditions*. New York: Harper & Bros., 1859.

Marmaduke, M.M., "Santa Fe Trail: M.M. Marmaduke Journal," ed. Francis A. Sampson. *Missouri Historical Review*, Vol. 6, No. 1 (October, 1911), pp. 1-10.

Parkman, Francis, Jr., *The California And Oregon Trail*. New York: William L. Allison Co., 18- (1849).

Pattie, James O., *The Personal Journal Of James O. Pattie Of Kentucky*. Cincinnati: E.H. Flint, 1833 (Reprint Ann Arbor: University of Michigan. Microfilm, Inc. 1966).

Porter, Clyde & Mae Reed Porter, *Matt Field On The Santa Fe Trail*, Ed. John E. Sunder. Norman: University of Oklahoma Press, 1960.

Russell, Marian Sloan. *Land Of Enchantment: Memoirs Of Marian Russell Along The Santa Fe Trail*. Reprint, Albuquerque: University of New Mexico Press, 1981.

Webb, James Josiah, *Adventures In The Santa Fe Trade, 1844–1847*. Ed. Ralph P. Bieber. Glendale: Arthur Clark Co., 1931.

Wilkins, James F., *An Artist On The Overland Trail, The Diary Of James F. Wilkins, 1849*. Ed. John McDermott. San Marino: The Huntington Library, 1968.

Index

Albert, James W., 33, 102, 130, 133, 134, 136, 138, 159, 160, 161, 171, 174, 175, 182, 199
Albuquerque, 25, 29
Alcove Spring, xxv
Alexander Majors House, 111, 204
Alvarez, Manuel, xxii
Apache, xxix, 9, 19, 20, 22
Apache Canyon, 25, 165
Arapaho, xxix, 12
Arkansas River, xxv, 13, 32, 141, 142, 143
Armijo, Manuel, xxxv
Arrow Rock, xxvii, 7, 10, 104, 203
Atchison & Topeka Railroad, 23, see also Atchison, Topeka, & Santa Fe
Atchison, Topeka, & Santa Fe, 24, 28, 29, 103, 141, 150
Aubry, Francis X., xxiv
Autograph Rock, 146

Baca/Bloom Pioneer Museum, 207
Baird, James, 5, 7
Bartleson-Bidwell Party, xxxvi
Battle of Glorieta Pass, 166, 211
Baudoin, Louison, 4
Beale, Edward, 58
Bear River, xxv
Bears, xiv
Becknell, Henry, 10
Becknell, William, xiv, xviii, xxxiii, xxxxvii, 6, 7, 10
Bellefontaine Cemetery, 190, 202
Bent, Charles, xxxv, 13, 17, 187, 212
Bent, Robert, 13
Bent, William, 13, 19, 21, 138, 188
Bent, George, xxxv, 13
Bent's New Fort, 19, 22, 58
Bent's Fort (Fort William), 13, 17, 133, 134, 135, 136, 188, 189
Bent's Old Fort National Historic Site, 207
Benton, Thomas, Hart, 6, 8, 104, 202, 203

Berryman, Reverend Mr., 113
Big Sandy Creek, 131
Big Spring, see also Santa Fe Spring, 104, 202
Big Timber (s), 19, 21, 131, 132
Bingham-Waggoner home, 112
Black Rock Desert, xxv, xxvi
Blockhouse - Fort Leavenworth, 106, 107
Blue River, 114
Blue Mountains, xxvi
Boiling Hot Springs, xxvi
Boone, Nathan, 3
Boone, Daniel, 3
Boone, Daniel, Jr., 4
Boonslick Trail, 3, 5
Boonville, 203
Brady Cabin, 110, 202
Brewerton, George, xxiii, 123, 128, 130, 144, 157, 183
Brown, William E., 215
Brown, Joseph C., 8, 32
Brown, Russell, & Co., 21
Brown's notebook, 33–47
Brown's map, 48–49
Brown Survey, see also Sibley Commission & survey, 32
Bryant, Edwin, 109, 114, 115
Buffalo, 123, 130
Bryam Brothers, xxi

Caddo (Caddoa) Creek, 131
Cailfornia Gold Rush, xvii, 19
Camp Nichols, xxxi, 27
Camp Mitchell, xxx
Camp on Pawnee Fort (Camp Alert), see also Fort Larned, 10
Canadian River, 149
Canby, Colonel E.R.S., 25
Cantonment Leavenworth, see also Fort Leavenworth, 10
Cantonment Loring, xxx
Carson River, xvv

Carson, Christopher "Kit", 9, 20, 27, 28, 104, 186, 203, 212
Cascades, xxvi
Cave Spring, 204
Chambers, Samuel, 5, 7
Chavez, Don Antonio Jose, 15
Chavez, Francisco, xxxvii
Cheyenne, xxix, 9, 24, 136, 138, 209
Chief Rabbit Ears, 209
Chief White Wolf, 19
Chief Black Kettle, 24
Chihuahua, xiii, xxi, 13
Child, Andrew, 56
Chivington, John, 24, 26
Cholera, 22
Chouteau, Augustus P., 5, 176
Chouteau's Island, 5, 12
Cimarron Cutoff, xxii, xxv, 14, 25, 28, 60, 70, 145, 151
Cimarron Valley, 145
Cimarron Crossing of Arkansas (Middle Crossing), 26
Cimarron, NM, 208
Civil War, xxii, 21, 24–26
Clamorgan, James, 4
Clark, William, 105
Cody, William (Buffalo Bill), 28
Colorado Gold Rush, xvii
Colorado Volunteers, 24
Columbia River, xxv
Comanche, xxix, 3, 9, 11, 12, 13, 14, 22, 138
Commerce, xvii
Commerce, value, xx, xxi
Conestoga (Pittsburgh) wagons, xxxi, xxxii, xxxiii, 198
Confederate Army, see also Civil War, 25
Confederate guerillas, 25
Conn Store, 117, 118, 196, 205
Conn, Malcolm, 117
Connor, Seymour, 216
Conrad, Howard Louis, 218
Coochatope Pass, 58
Cooke, Philip St. George, 15, 16
Cooper, Benjamin, 7
Cooper, Captain, 116

Cooper, Stephen, 7
Cottonwood Crossing, xxiii
Council Grove, xxvii, 9, 11, 26, 116, 205
Council Grove - name, 9, 116
Council Grove Oak, 116, 205
Council Grove Treaty, 205
Courthouse Square, see also Independence Square, 10
Cow Creek, 70, 119
Crossing the Arkansas, 142, 143, 144

Dana, Charles, 109
Dary, David, 218
De Mun, Jules, 5
"Dearborns", xxxiii, 8
Delgado, F.B., xxxviii, 146
Denver, 27
Devil's Rock, xxvii, 27
Diamond Spring, xxv, 10
Diaries, 60, 69, 70
Diocese of Santa Fe, 22
Diseases, xxvii, xxviii
Distances, xxii, xxiii
Dodge City, 18, 28
Donner Party, xxvii
Donoho, Mary A. xxxvii
Donoho, Nary Watt Dodson, xxxvii
Double Hot Springs, xxv
Double Wells, xxvi
Draft animals, xxxv, xxxvi
Dry Turkey Creek, 9
Duffus, Robert, 216

Ellsberg-Amberg caravan, 173
Emigrant Springs, xxv
Emory, William H., 33, 54, 71
Emporia, 28
Escudero, Dr. Manuel, xxxviii
Exchange Hotel, 181

Field, Matt, 120, 121, 131, 139, 217
Fitzhugh's Mill, 114, 204
Fitzpatrick, Thomas, 22
Flar (Upper) Spring, 146
Forsyth, Thomas, xxxv
Forts, see also specific fort, xxx

Fort Aubry, xxxi
Fort Atkinson, xxxi, 21, 22
Fort Bridger, xxx
Fort Cascades, xxx
Fort Caspar (Platte Bridge Station), xxx
Fort Churchill, xxx
Fort Dalles (Drum), xxx
Fort Dodge, xxxi, 26, 129
Fort Ellsworth, xxxi
Fort Floyd, xxx
Fort Gibson, 14
Fort Grattan, xxx
Fort Hoskins, xxx
Fort Kearny, xxx
Fort Lane, xxx
Fort Laramie (Fort William), 13, 14
Fort Laramie, xxx
Fort Laramie Treaty (Horse Creek Treaty), 22
Fort Larned, xxxi, 26, 124, 125, 126, 206
Fort Larned National Historic Site, 206
Fort Leavenworth, xiv, xxx, xxxi, 12, 17, 106, 204, 205
Fort Lyons I, xxxi, 24
Fort Lyons II, xxi
Fort MacKay, see Fort Mann
Fort Mann, xxi, 17, 21
Fort Marcy, xxxi, 182
Fort Massachusetts, 58
Fort McPherson (Cottonwood), xxx
Fort Osage, xxxi, 4, 9, 10, 71, 105, 116, 203
Fort Riley, xxxi, 22
Fort Union, first or log fort, 152, 153
Fort Union, xxxi, 25, 151, 152, 153, 154, 155, 156, 210, 211
Fort Union National Monument, 210, 211
Fort Umpqua, xxx
Fort Vancouver, xxx, 185
Fort Wise, see also Fort Lyon, xxvii, xxxi, 24
Fort Yamhill, xxx
Fort Zarah, 26

Forty-Mile Desert, xxv, xxvi
"Four mule wagon", xxxiv
Fraker, Charles, 210
Franklin, MO, 5, 6, 8, 203
Franzwa, Gregory, 214, 215
Fremont, John Charles, 9, 32, 33, 102, 136, 137
Freight wagons, xxxii, 180, 197

Gardner, KS, xvii
Garrard, Lewis, 217
Gila River, xxxix
Gila River Route, xviii, 19
Glorietta (Martin) Pass, 25, 165, 166
Gold, xxvii
Gold rush, xxxvii
Governor's Palace, 173, 176, 212
Great Salt Lake desert, xxv
"Great Migration", xxxvi
Great Bend, 26, 28, 32, 70, 143
Gregg, Josiah, xiii, xix, xx, xxi, xxiii, 14, 15, 32, 57, 58, 69, 70, 102, 119, 122, 127, 130, 147, 148, 149, 159, 165, 170, 172, 189, 216
Grier, Captain, 20
Guidebooks, see also specific guides, 55–60
Gutierrez, Jose, xxxviii

Hafen, Leroy, 218
Hall, Jacob, 20
Harris, H. H., 6
Hastings, Lansford, 56
Hays City, 28
Heger, Joseph, 152
Hickok, Wild Bill, xiv
Hill, Thomas, 117, 118
Hines, Celinda E., 113
Hoehne, CO, 138
Holladay, Ben, xxi, xxxiv
Holliday, Cyrus K., 23
Hopi Indian Snake Dancers, 103
Horn, Hosea, 56
Hough, John, 207
Humboldt (Marys) River, xxv
Hunt, Samuel, 199
Huston, Joseph, 104

Independence Square & Courthouse, 109
Independence Spring, 110
Independence, MO, xvii, xxiv, 10, 19, 110, 204
Indians, xviii, xxix, 11, 14, 18, 22, 23, 24, 26
Inman, Henry, 216
Irrigation, 142, 143

Jackson, William Henry, 108
Jackson, President Andrew, 12
James, Thomas, 7
"Jarvis Creek", see also Chavez, 15
Jefferson National Expansion Memorial, 202
Johnson's ranch, 26, 212
Jones Spring, see also Diamond Spring, 10
Jornada, xxvi, 7, 13, 14, 70, 146

Kansa (Kaw) Indians, 9
Kansas Pacific Railroad, 27, 28
Kansas State Historical Society, 113
Kaw Mission, 117, 205
Kearney, Stephen Watts, xxix, 16, 19, 33, 102, 133, 187, 193, 202, 204, 207
Kelsey, Nancy, xxxvi
Kelsey, Ann, xxxvi
Kendall, George Wilkins, 15
Kimball, Stanley B., 215
Kiowa, xxix, 3, 9, 22
Kit Carson, CO, 28
Koziowski ranch, 212

La Junta, xxv, 28
La Lande, Bapiste, 3
Lamme, Mr., 12
Lamy, Jean Bapiste, 22
Land grant bill, 23
Las Vegas, 157, 158
Last Chance Store, 118, 205
Lavender, David, 218
Lawrence, KS, 28
Lewis & Clark, 4
Lisa, Manuel, 4

Log Courthouse, 111, 204
Lost Spring, xxv
Louisiana Purchase, 4
Louisiana Territory, 105
Lower Cimarron Spring, 146

Magoffin, James, 17
Magoffin, Samuel, xxi, 16, 190, 202
Magoffin, Susan (cousin), 191
Magoffin, Susan, xiii, xiv, xxi, xxvii, xxxvii, 16, 69, 70, 114, 119, 121, 127, 133, 139, 160, 162, 165, 190, 191, 202, 207, 217
Mail coach attack, 151
Mail service, 20
Majors, Alexander, xxi, xxvii, 8, 18, 23, 111, 194, 218
Majors, Benjamin, 8
Mallet brothers, Paul & Pierre, 3
"Map of the Western Territory", 50
"Map to New Mexico and The Southern Rocky Mountains", 52–53
Marcy, Randolph, xxxvi, 60
Marmaduke, Meredith M., xix, xx, xxxiii, 8, 10
Martin, Gene & Mary, 216
Mathewson, William (Buffalo Bill), 28, 119
Maxwell, Lucien, 208
McBride, George C., 27
McCoy, William, 20
McCoy, Isaac, 13
McDaniel, "Captain" John, 15
McKnight, Robert, 5
McKnight, John, xxix, 7
McLavanhan, James, 5
McNees (?), xxix, 11
McNee's Crossing, 11, 114
McNees, Samuel G., 11
Means, Captain John, 11
Meline, Colonel J.F., xxiv
Merriwether, David, 5
Mexican merchants, xxxvii, xxxviii
Mexican War, xxi, xxix, 13, 15, 16, 18
Mexican Independence, xviii

Mexican trade restrictions, xix
Mexico City, xviii, 15
Middle Springs, xxvi
Middle Crossing, 142, 144
"Milepost zero", 9, 71
Military, xxi
Minor Park, 114, 204
"Missouri mules", 7
Monroe (Munroe), Daniel, xxix, 11
Monroe, President James, 8
Mora, 157, 211
Morgan, Dale, 217
Mormon Battalion, xxix, 17
Morrison, William, 3
Mountain Branch, xxii, xv, 33, 60, 70, 133
Munkres, James, 117
Murphy Wagons, xxxiii, xxxiv, 196
Murphy, Joseph, xxxiii
Museum of New Mexico, 103

National Park Service, 162, 163, 164
National Frontier Trails Center, 112, 195
Navaho, xxix
Neosho River, 9, 116
"New Philadelphia", 10
Newton, KS, 28

Old Fort Kearny (Child), xxx
Old Spanish Trail, xviii, 19, 58
"Oldest house", 177, 212
Olivia, Leo & Bonita, 217
Oregon-California Trails, xvii, xxii, xxiv, xxv, xxvi, xxvii, xxix, xxx, xxxi, xxxii, xxxvi, xxxvii, 55, 56, 106, 204
Oregon-California Trails Association, xv
Osage Indians, 9
Otero, Miquel, xxxvii

Parish Church, 180, 182, 212
Parkman, Fancis, 107
Patterson, James, 5
Pawnee, 9, 11, 14
Pawnee Fork, 123, 124

Pawnee Rock, 120, 121, 122, 205, 206
Peck, W.G., 32, 33
Pecos National Monument, 211
Pecos River, 159, 160
Pecos Ruins, 161, 162, 163, 164
Perea, Joaquin, xxxvii
Perea, Francisco, xxxvii
Pigeon Ranch, 26, 166, 167, 168, 169, 212
Pike, Zebulon, 4, 5, 9, 176
Pike's Peak, xviii, 4
Pilot Peak, xxv
Pittsburgh, PA, xxi
Platte River, xxv
Pony Express, xxiv
Post Office Oak, 205
Prairie, xiv, 115, 157, 158
Prairie dogs, 127, 128, 206
Price, Sterling, 17
Purcell (Pursley), James, 3, 23
Pyron, Charles L., 26

Quaife, Milton, 218
Quantrill's Raiders, 26
"Queen of the Pantry Flour", 112

Rabbit ears, 147
Rabbit Hole Springs, xxvi
Railroads, xxii, xxiii, 22, 24, 27, 28, 208
Raton Pass, 7, 13, 27, 28
Raton Mountains, xiv, xxvi, xxvii, 70, 137, 139, 140, 141, 207
Rattlesnakes, 120, 121, 127, 149
Reading, Pierson Barton, 113
Rice Farm, 204
Riley, Bennet, xxxv, 12
Rittenhouse, Jack D., 217
"Road Wagon", xxxiii
Robidoux, Antonio, xxiii
Robbers, xxvii
Rock Crossing, 149
Round Mound, 148, 149
Russell, William, 23
Russell, Majors, & Wadel, xxi, 18, 194

Russell, Marian, xiii, xxxvii, 27, 217

Sam, James Sheperd's slave, 111
Samuel Barlow, xxvii
San Miquel, 159, 160
San Miquel Chapel, 177, 178, 180, 190, 212
San Francisco Street, 180, 181
Sand Creek, 12, 145
Sand Creek Massacre, 24
Santa Fe Trail Center Museum, 112, 206
Santa Fe Plaza, 173, 180, 212
Santa Fe Spring, see also Big Spring, 203
Santa Fe Opera, 212
Santa Fe Trail Association, 217
Santa Clara Spring, xxv, 210
Santa Fe, 3, 4, 6, 8, 17, 24, 25, 29, 58, 170–182, 212
Sapello River, 151
Sappington, Dr. John, xxvii
Sawyer, Lorenzo, xxiv
Scurry, Colonel William R., 16
Sedwick, John, 24
Shawnee Methodist Mission, 113, 204
Shepherd's farm, James, 109
Sheridan, Philip, 26
Sibley Commission, see also Brown Survey, 32
Sibley Survey, see also Brown Survey, 57, 203
Sibley, H.H., 25
Sibley, George Chaplin, 8, 10, 32, 57, 69, 70, 71, 110, 116, 120, 127, 203, 212
Sierra Nevada, xxvi
Simmons, Marc, 214, 217
"Six mule wagon", xxiv
Skaggs, James, 216
Slough, John P., 26
Smith, Ira, 14
Smith, Rueben, 5
Smith, Jedediah, xxvi, 12, 13, 146, 185, 209

Smith, Fitzpatrick, Jackson, Sublette caravan, 12
Smoky Hill Trail, xxxi, 23
Snake River, xxv
Snively, Jacob, 15
Snow storms, xxiii, xxvii, 7, 18, 19, 195
Spalding, Eliza, xxxvi
Spanish Fever, 23
Spanish Peaks, 137, 138
Speyer, Albert, xxii, 16
Spratt, Bertram, 20
Springer livery stable, 150
St. Francis Cathedral, 180, 183, 212
St. Louis, MO, 202
St. James Hotel, 208
St. Varain, Ceran, 13
Stage service, xxviii, 17, 20, 23
Star Fort, see also Fort Union, 25
State Buffalo Preserve, 130, 206
Storms, 18, 19, 123
Storrs, Augustus, 8, 9
Street, Franklin, 56
Sublettes Flat, xxv
Summer Colonel, 21

Taos, xviii, 9, 17, 183, 187, 212
Taos Revolt, 183, 187
Texans, 14, 15
Texas Santa Fe Expedition, 15
"The Caches", 7, 18, 32, 70, 71
The Rookery, 107
Timpas Creek, 137
Toll Road, 27, 28, 192, 208
Topeka, 28
Trade restrictions, xxxv, 14, 16
Trade goods, xix, xxii
Traders-Hispanic & Mexican, xxxvii, xxxviii, xxxix, 146
Travel time, xxiii, xxiv
Travelers, xxxvi
Treaty of Guadalupe Hildago, 18
Trinidad, 27, 28, 207
Trukee River, xxv
Turkey Creek, 209

U.S. Army Command and General
    Staff College, 204
Upper (Cimarron) Crossing, 5
Utes, 20

Valle, Alexander, 168
Vial, Pedro, 3
Viscarra, Colonel Antonio, 5, 12

Waggoner, Peter, 112
Waggoner-Gates Mill, 112
Wagon Bed Spring National Historic
    Landmark, 209
Wagon Bed Springs (Lower
    Springs), xxvi, 146, 209
Wagon Mound, 20, 151, 210
Wagon caravan - typical, xxiv
Wagons - description, xxxi, xxxii,
    197, 198
"Wah-To-Yah", 137
Waldo, David, 20, 21
Walker, John, 116
Walker, Joseph Reddeford, 8
Walnut Creek, 14, 26
Ware, Joseph, 56
Warfield, "Texas Colonel", 15
Warm Springs, xxv
Watrous (La Junta), 151, 157, 210
Webb, James Josiah, xix, xxxv, 16,
    142, 165, 170, 217
West Las Animus, 28
Westport, xvii, 13
Westport Landing, 108
Wet & dry routes, 129
Wharton, Captain Clifton, 14
Wheeler Expedition, 178
White, James M. & family, 19
Whitman, Dr. Marcus, xxxvi
Whitman, Narcissa, xxxvi
Wilkins, James, 106
Willamette Valley, xviii
Willow Spring, xxv
Willow Bar, xxiii
Wilson family, 25
"Windwagon" Thomas, 22
Wise, Governor Henry, 24
Wittick, Ben, 102, 103, 164

Women, xxxvii, xxxviii
Wooton, "Uncle Dick" Richens Lacy,
    xxiv, xxvii, xxxiv, 27, 28, 192
Wyandotte, 27

Younger family, 110